One Candle
at a Time

Ron Berger

One Candle at a Time

Published by:

berger publishing

berger publishing

Rancho Belago, CA 92555
Email - mail@ronberger.com
Web Page - www.ronberger.com

Printed in the USA
ISBN 13 - 978-0-9799257-5-7
ISBN 10 - 0-9799257-5-4
First printing
Library of Congress Control
Number:2010911205

Ron's other books -

The House That Ron Built
(1-4137-8605-7) (978-1-4137-8605-7)
PublishAmerica, LLC
Are You Being Served Yet?
(1-4241-2485-9) (978-14241-2485-5)
PublishAmerica, LLC
P-NUT, The Love of a Dog
(1-59824-303-9) (978-1-59824-303-1)
E-Book Time, LLC
"Normal" MAYDAY
(0-9799257-0-3) (978-0-9799257-0-2)
berger publishing
Time for TEA
(0-9799257-1-1) (978-0-9799257-1-9)
berger publishing
Growing Old is a FULL-TIME JOB
(0-9799257-2-X) (978-0-9799257-2-6)
berger publishing
Time for MORE TEA
(0-9799257-3-8) (978-0-9799257-3-3)
berger publishing
Time for STILL MORE TEA
(0-9799257-4-6) (978-0-9799257-4-0)
berger publishing

Author's Note:

E-mail messages and article clips used in this book are started with (**) and ended with (****) with credit given if the author and/or source is known.

I beseech everyone, who reads this book, to get involved and to lend their voice in turning this country around. I am not a member of the "radical right" or the "right wing conspiracy" but after reading this you will find that the "radical left" and the "left wing conspiracy" is growing fast. I could write much more, but I don't want you to get bored. I love this country and only want to see it survive.
This book shows how one person can start a "wildfire". We need to light enough candles for the world to see that we are the
"Light of the World"

Join the TEA PARTY while it is still possible.

Contents

About the author   6

Introduction   9

In The Beginning   14

One Candle   39

Twelve Candles   52

Israel   59

Immigration   82

Arizona   144

Our Government   165

More Surprises   279

Summation   307

ABOUT THE AUTHOR

Coming from a small town in Wisconsin, I was never exposed to much in the political realm. My dad was a Democrat, mainly because he was a union worker for the Electric Company, and he only looked for his benefits. My mother was a Republican (I think). Only one election did I get involved enough to actually offer my voting advise. It was 1948 when I heard Harry Truman talk and it made much more sense to me than Thomas Dewey that I advised my mother to vote for Truman. I don't know if she ever did, but Mr Truman was the last Democrat that made sense to me.

The election of 1952 was a no-brainer as far as I was concerned. I really felt sorry for Adlai Stevenson - and then for him to campaign against General Eisenhower twice in four years was too much. Even the Democratic party tried to get Ike to run on their ticket in 1951. He was my Commander-in-Chief while I was in the USAF and I was proud of that fact.

My political life started to take shape when I was hired by a builder in California. That family was 100% Republican and you had better be also if you wanted to work for them. I didn't have to make any adjustment in my thinking and was on board with them from the first day. Nixon was our man and Kennedy was not. The next election in 1964 was Goldwater and not Johnson. We all know how those elections turned out.

During most Local, State and Federal elections I would automatically vote Republican. That doesn't mean that I thought they were better, but rather it was just easier. During the election of 1992 I broke that pattern and voted for Ross Perot. After he fell flat on his butt, I stopped voting altogether. I really couldn't tell the good from the bad. Oh, I had feelings, but figured that my vote didn't count anyway so why go through the hassle?

The last election between Obama and McCain really got me worked up. Not only did I feel this country now was going down the wrong path, but I felt an urgency about doing something about it. That's what most people felt, but didn't know what they should do about it. After about a year of receiving Obama bashing emails I realized that there has to be some truth to it. Then came the "Tea Party Brigades". I have never seen the general public so worked up and so wanting to turn this country around and take the control back from the Obama administration.

Now that a year plus has gone by with B. O. (Barack Obama) in charge, the meaning of "change" has really sunk in. He claimed that the USA was the best country in the world and he wanted to "change" it from the last administration. We now know that his change means socialism.

Lord, save us from those that think they know more than our founding fathers on how to run this country. This is the time for a complete change in Washington, DC.

This is TEA TIME!

Ron Berger 8

INTRODUCTION

During the writing of my previous three TEA books I have become incensed by the actions of "our" government. We are increasingly moving to the Socialistic side and it is not in keeping with our Constitution. More and more evidence is coming my way that just begs me to speak out.

My "Time for TEA", "Time for MORE TEA" and "Time for STILL MORE TEA" books have talked about the problems we are facing. We really have three enemies that are already here and are actively moving against us.

Until now, I'm sure most of you believe that we are safe and have nothing to fear. Let me warn you that is not the case and our ability to fight back is being severely hampered and actually propagated by the liberal faction of our government.

The President and Congress have steered our movement in the direction of bankruptcy and Islam. BO has even said that if push comes to shove, he will stand with Islam.

Our children and their children are now saddled with the largest deficit in history. You will be punished if you don't sign up for ObamaCare and you wont be able to sell your house until you have a permit, issued by the government to make sure you are in compliance with all the laws.

That is just two of the problems that face us and are illegal, but have been signed into law by BO. Fixing the immigration problem will be fixed simply by making all the illegals, citizens. Still, being illegals, they have more benefits than citizens.

Our three "true enemies" are the Islamic terrorists, the Mexicans and our own government. You know about the terrorists and you probably still feel that only the "odd ball" terrorist does something in the USA. The people doing things like "the shoe bomber", "the underwear bomber" and the "times square bomber" are "home grown" and there are many more where they came from. There are Islamic cells that are actively recruiting members to do damage to our country.

France, England and Germany are already facing these problems and are frozen on what to do. Europe is already being over-whelmed and will be lost to our cause in the very near future.

Mexico is a silent enemy. They actually support sending illegals to our country so they don't have to deal with them. They also castigate us for sealing our borders to these illegals. Arizona has come under great criticism for the laws they recently passed, both by Mexico and BO.

The Mexican cities closest to the border are complaining that they can't handle all their citizens that are coming back. Isn't that a shame?

Our third enemy is our own government including the President and those liberals in Congress. BO is the worst occupier of the White House since Carter and the liberal leaders in the Senate and the House just follow him around like a puppy, bowing to every whim he murmurs. We have the largest bunch of spineless traitors that ever gathered in one place.

This book deals more with how to combat the evil forces that are rearing their ugly head. Needless to say, one person will not make a difference and a thousand - barely noticeable, but, we have to start somewhere.

The "Tea Parties" are doing a fine job. Still, many people still can't believe that what we face is not just another problem that will iron itself out as time goes buy. This problem is a "life changing" one that requires us to actively participate in eradicating.

We are at war with terrorists in Iraq and Afghanistan, but fail to see the war that needs fighting right here in the USA. This war is one that will lead to our ultimate destruction if we just sit back and "hope for the best".

Now is the time to act and rid ourselves of our enemies right in our own country. We must call upon the One that helped us create the best country to live in and who we are trying to ignore with the help of our government.

Ron

In The Beginning

John 8:12-30 Jesus: Light of the World part 3 by Richard Cimino

We began our study of these words by looking at the theme of light through the Old Testament and into John's Gospel. We found the first mention of this theme and concept at the beginning of the Book of Beginnings — Genesis. There (Genesis 1:3) God created light and then separated the light from the darkness. From that point forward — the theme of light — and of God separating light from

Ron Berger 14

darkness — becomes a metaphor through the Bible of what God does in human lives and in human history. This theme hyperlinks itself throughout the rest of the Scriptures. If you missed the first 2 studies of this passage I would encourage you to get the media resources (metrocalvary.org) for those studies to get the theological concepts wrapped up in the term LIGHT.

We saw that these words were framed against the backdrop of the the Feast of Booths — one of the three great feasts in the Jewish calendar; in particular the backdrop of the opening night of the feast. On that first night of the Feast of Booths there was a ceremony called The Illumination of the Temple. In that ceremony they lit a series of massive candelabras — the brilliant light they produced symbolized all of the Old Testament theology about God being light — His Word being light — walking with Him in the light.

With that ceremony still being fresh in the minds and hearts of His audience on the Temple Mount Jesus declared — John 8:12 ...."I am the light of the world. Jesus — in the vicinity of those massive candelabras — says I am the light of the world. Again — one of the seven I AM statements of Jesus in the Gospel of John. Jesus is saying that HE is — in and of Himself — the one who gives the LIGHT of the presence of God.

John 8:12 ....Whoever follows me will not walk in darkness, but will have the light of life." Jesus not only says that He is — in and of Himself — the source of LIGHT in this dark world; He says that the ONLY way to EXPERIENCE that Light and BE in that light is to Follow HIM!

We spent virtually the whole of our time together last Sunday walking around in the personal and powerful implications of that word FOLLOW. We learned that this Greek word that had five different usages. This one Greek word is FILLED with powerful and personal implications! It's a Greek word that had five different usages.

1.) It was used in speaking of a soldier following his captain. It's a military term that meant there was someone in authority over you who had the right to command conduct and action from you — and discipline you for disobedience.

2.) The word was also used in speaking of a slave accompanying his master. We saw how the Scriptures say that everyone is a slave. You're either a slave to

Sin, Satan and death; Or you're a slave to Jesus, Grace and Life. You either belong to Satan or you belong to God. You either belong to sin or you belong to grace. You either belong to death or you belong to life. You are not free — You are a slave. The question is — Who is your master? Who owns you? Who possesses you?

3.) The third use of this word was to refer to a person following the counsel of a wise teacher. Its use implied that for all of our academic and scientific and technological advances — we are all lost — we are all stumbling around in darkness. Jesus says that if we follow Him we won't WALK in darkness. Paul tells us (1 Corinthians 1:24) that Jesus is the very wisdom of God. Following Jesus means that we are following Him as our teacher.

4.) It was also used to speak of a citizen obeying the laws of his king and his kingdom. To follow Jesus means that we recognize Jesus as King. He sits on the throne — we are his faithful subjects. Following Jesus means that we do what Jesus says because the King and His glory supersedes the subjects, that God's glory is more important than our own.

5.) William Barclay states the last meaning with great clarity — Quote: William Barclay —The Christian is the man who has understood the meaning of the teaching of Christ.... He takes the message into his mind and understands, receives the words into his memory and remembers, and hides them in his heart and obeys.

THAT IS WHAT IT MEANS TO FOLLOW JESUS. It means that we recognize the authority of Jesus as general — as king — as teacher. We noted that THAT kind of authority totally undoes any churchy or romantic concept of claiming to follow Jesus! Do I really follow Jesus — As king? As Master/Lord? As God? As judge? As ruler? As commander? As teacher? NOW WE COME TO THE RESPONSE OF THE CROWD. Everyone in this room will find themselves identifying with one of these 2 groups. The Pharisees challenged him. So the Pharisees said to him, "You are bearing witness about yourself; your testimony is not true." The Pharisees didn't like the tone of authority in the words of Jesus — So they challenged His authority. In essence — "You're appearing as your own witness — that invalidates your testimony." You see in the Old Testament God established the rule for valid testimony — Deuteronomy 19:15 "A single witness shall not suffice .... Only on the evidence of two witnesses or of three witnesses shall a charge be established. That's makes great sense — You wouldn't let somebody get off on his or her own testimony. Hey, did you back into my car in the parking lot? No! Do you have any witnesses? No, just take my word for it. I'm not going to take your word for it. You have a vested interest in telling the lie. So these guys are saying — You say you're the light of the world? Bring in some witnesses. Jesus answered, "Even if I do bear witness about myself, my testimony is true, for I know where I came from and where I am going, but you do not know where I come from or where I am going. Jesus says — You know what? God doesn't need witnesses. God is THE truth teller. When God says something He doesn't need to haul in a bunch of other people to support him. I'm God — My testimony is true in and of itself — but you have no idea where I come from or where I am going.

You judge according to the flesh; You judge by human standards — I judge no one. Yet even if I do judge, my judgment is true, for it is not I alone who judge, but I and the Father who sent me. 5 Jesus now brings the Father forward as a corroborating witness — the Sent One calls on the Sender. 17In your Law it is written that the testimony of two men is true. I am the one who bears witness about myself, and the Father who sent me bears witness about me." You want a witness? How about God the Father. Let's bring Him to the bar and He can put His hand on His own book and He can make an oath that He'll tell the whole truth and nothing but the truth — so help Himself! Do you want a witness? How about God, the Father? Jesus says — Here's your two witnesses — Me and My Father!

And then they try to insult Jesus. They said to him therefore, "Where is your Father?" They are inferring that Jesus was illegitimate! Where's your dad? Oh — That's right — you don't even know who your father is. Your mother was a loose woman and you don't even know who Your dad is! That's what people thought about Jesus and His mother throughout the course of His life. These guys thought they had just shredded on Jesus by outing Him as illegitimate. But God Incarnate has some radical words for these religious professionals! Jesus answered, "You know neither me nor my Father. If you knew me, you would know my Father also." These words he spoke in the treasury, as he taught in the temple; but no one arrested him, because his hour had not yet come.

Your problem is you don't know God! Lots of people will say — Well I don't necessarily buy into Jesus — but I really believe in God. Jesus says that we can't say that!

Jesus says, "If you knew me you'd know the father." You cannot know the Father except through the Son.

John 14:6 Jesus said to him, "I am the way, and the truth, and the life. No one comes to the Father except through me. 20 These words he spoke in the treasury, as he taught in the temple; but no one arrested him, because his hour had not yet come. It wasn't yet time for him to die. On a number of occasions John points out that human attempts to kill Jesus were thwarted because their plans did not conform to God's timetable for the suffering and death of Jesus.

John 12:23-24; 27; 31-32 And Jesus answered them, "The hour has come for the Son of Man to be glorified. Truly, truly, I say to you, unless a grain of wheat falls into the earth and dies, it remains alone; but if it dies, it bears much fruit....."Now is my soul troubled. And what shall I say? 'Father, save me from this hour'? But for this purpose I have come to this hour..... 31 Now is the judgment of this world; now will the ruler of this world be cast out.

And I, when I am lifted up from the earth, will draw all people to myself."

So he said to them again, "I am going away, and you will seek me, and you will die in your sin. Where I am going, you cannot come." KEY INSIGHT: The word SIN is singular. QUOTE: D.A. Carson New Bible commentary — this would refer to the sin of rejecting the Messiah. By rejecting Jesus they were rejecting the one and only remedy for your sin.

So the Jews said, "Will he kill himself, since he says, 'Where I am going, you cannot come'?" They think he's talking about killing himself. Jesus is talking about his death and resurrection and return to the Father. But he continued. He said to them, "You are from below; I am from above. You are of this world; I am not of this world. Jesus points out the infinite gulf between Himself and fallen man — even the most religious of men! You live in the darkness. I am from above — I bring the light. You are of this world — dark. I am not of this world — light. If you will not bring your sin into my light, you will die in your sin.

I told you that you would die in your sins, for unless you believe that I am he you will die in your sins." QUOTE: A.T. Robertson, Word Pictures in the New Testament. Jesus can mean either "unless you believe that I am from above" (verse 23), "unless you believe that that I am the one sent from the Father or the Messiah" (7:18, 28), "unless you believe that I am the Light of the World" (8:12), "unless you believe that I am the Deliverer from the bondage of sin" — You will die in your sins. HUGE INSIGHT: The Greek text has simply — Unless you believe that I am — period. A.T. Robertson notes that — The phrase occurs three times in this chapter (8:24, 28, and especially 58). VERSE 58 - Jesus said to them, "Truly, truly, I say to you, before Abraham was, I am."

Robertson also says that the Old Testament scriptures used the language in relationship to Yahweh/Jehovah (Deut. 32:39 Isa. 43:10) Jesus is asserting that He is the great 'I am' of the OT (Ex. 3:14). He is declaring that He is the Self-Existent God of Israel! Jesus is saying to this crowd — Unless you recognize Me as God — And bring your sin into the light of who I am — and into the light of my nature as messiah and redeemer — you will die in your sin.

THIS IS HUGE — Unless we step into the light of God — as revealed in the face of Jesus Christ (2 Corinthians 4:6) — we can never know our sin — and as a result we will never see our need for a savior. QUOTE: D.A. Carson, Scandalous — ....the hardest truth to get across to this generation is what the Bible says about sin..... There is so much in our culture that teaches us that we define our own sins, either individually or socially.... We live in an age where the one wrong thing to say is that somebody else is wrong.... we all have our own independent points of view, and we look at things from the perspective of our own small interpretive communities. What is sin to one group is not sin to another group. But not only does the Bible insist that there is such a thing as sin, it insists that the heart of its ugly offensiveness is its horrible odiousness to God—how it offends God.

So they said to him, "Who are you?" Literally — "You, who are you?" He had virtually claimed to be the Messiah; equal in nature with God. They want to pin him down and to charge him with blasphemy. Jesus said to them, "Just what I have been telling you from the beginning.

I have much to say about you and much to judge, I could sit here and judge you for a really long time — I have a lot to say about your judgment, but I'll answer your question. But he who sent me is true, and I declare to the world what I have heard from him."

They did not understand that he had been speaking to them about the Father. So Jesus said to them, "When you have lifted up the Son of Man, Jesus is pointing to His death — being lifted up on a cross outside of the walls of Jerusalem. then you will know that I am he, and that I do nothing on my own authority, but speak just as the Father taught me.

And he who sent me is with me. He has not left me alone, for I always do the things that are pleasing to him."

What a sweet and succinct summary of the life of Jesus — I just do what pleases him. THAT is what living under the light of God looks like — just doing what pleases Him. And in this moment we see that a lot of people — powerful and influential RELIGIOUS people reject this. They hate Jesus for what He has to say. They are opposing Jesus because Jesus has called them into his light so that their darkness would be exposed. In the face of this rejection John adds these words — words that give us a glimmer of hope — As he was saying these things, many believed in him. While the religious movers and shakers were rejecting Jesus — There were people listening in on this whole exchange who said — Well then, that's it. I'm making my choice right here and now — I'm going to live in the light of God.

Here's my sin, here's what I've done. Here's how messed up I've been. Here is my pride. Here are all of my futile attempts at trying to be a good person and hold my life together. I'm in. By the way — when you are sharing Jesus with a group of people — and they are shutting down — don't limit the Lord. You never know who is listening in — the person or persons on the fringe that are drinking it in and are going to step in to the light! So there were MANY who put their faith in him, who said — I trust you. I don't know where this is going. I don't know what you're going to do with me — but I trust You! Whatever you say — that's what I'm going to do. You do whatever pleases the Father. I'll do whatever pleases you. That way I'll be doing whatever pleases the Father.

It is so amazing — so incredible — to step into the light of God.

AS WE CLOSE — I want you to hear what happens to those who step into and abide in the light of God. And if I weren't reading to you from the inspired, inerrant, infallible Word of God, all of this would be unbelievable.

Acts 26:18 to open their eyes, so that they may turn from darkness to light and from the power of Satan to God, that they may receive forgiveness of sins and a place among those who are sanctified by faith in me.

Here is what God does for you the moment you step into the light of God —

You are delivered from the power of Satan to God. Your sins are forgiven. You are cleansed, and set apart unto God — your life is transformed by the grace and the power of God and his light.

2 Corinthians 4:4 In their case the god of this world has blinded the minds of the unbelievers, to keep them from seeing the light of the gospel of the glory of Christ, who is the image of God.... For God, who said, "Let light shine out of darkness," has shone in our hearts to give the light of the knowledge of the glory of God in the face of Jesus Christ. When you step into the light of God and you remain in the light of God you get the privilege of seeing clearly the Gospel of Christ, what he has accomplished on your behalf. The whole world looks at Christ in the story and is blinded and does not see it, and you get the joy of seeing the Gospel and the glory of Christ who is the image of God. You see Jesus for who he is and what he has done.

2 Corinthians 4:6 For God, who said, "Let light shine out of darkness," has shone in our hearts to give the light of the knowledge of the glory of God in the face of Jesus Christ. The light of God is not just

something that operates apart from us. It is a personal and relational knowledge of God that is placed into the very essence of who we are.

Ephesians 5:8-9 for at one time you were darkness, but now you are light in the Lord. Walk as children of light (for the fruit of light is found in all that is good and right and true),

As you live in the light of God you discover new life by God's grace. It is governed by righteousness — by that which is right by God. Truth comes so you no longer need to live in lies and in darkness.

There is goodness instead of selfishness and wickedness and rebellion. ALL of that by living under the light of God. Don't misunderstand me — We will not be perfect in this life — but at that same time I do believe that as we live under the light of God — we begin to discover that the darkness bothers us as much as the light used to — because even as we used to be accustomed to the dark — now in Jesus we have become accustomed to goodness, righteousness and truth. And though we are tempted by that darkness

— we now see it for what it really is and it is distasteful to the child of God.

1 Thessalonians 5:5 For you are all children of light, children of the day. We are not of the night or of the darkness. Following Jesus — walking in the light of life causes you to recognize that you are a son or a daughter, an adopted member of God's family, and that God is your father.

Titus 1:2-3 in hope of eternal life, which God, who never lies, promised before the ages began and at the proper time manifested in his word through the preaching with which I have been entrusted by the command of God our Savior; Part of what you receive as a benefit of God's grace under his light is the preaching of his Word. As you remain in the light — God will continue to reveal himself to you through the preaching of his Word.

1 Peter 2:9 But you are a chosen race, a royal priesthood, a holy nation, a people for his own possession, that you may proclaim the excellencies of him who called you out of darkness into his marvelous light.

This is so RADICAL — As a bi-product of living under the light of God you are a new people, part of the work and family and plan of the kingdom of God. In the Old Testament the priests served God in the Temple. Following Jesus, the Light of the World, brings us into the place of serving God in the House of God — the Body of Christ.

This is HUGE — If you are a follower of Jesus you have been given work to do as a priest serving your God. You now have this wonderful opportunity to give praise to His glory for those ways that His light has flooded into your life and transformed you. ALL of your darkness was forgiven. ALL of your darkness was healed. The darkness was overcome. Christ showed up. And I now get to praise him and work for Jesus!

1 John 2:9-10 Whoever says he is in the light and hates his brother is still in darkness. Whoever loves his brother abides in the light, and in him there is no cause for stumbling. If you live under the light then, you love the people of God and when they sin against you — you extend the same light and grace and forgiveness of the gospel that God, in Christ,

has given to you. Living like results in there being no darkness between you and others in your relationships — because now the light of God is coming through you to permeate that space that has separated you and that other person, and now you are reconciled as the light of Jesus in and through you comes into that darkness and overcomes it by God's grace. And if you don't live that way you are not exercising the beautiful power of the light that Christ has given you.

FINALLY — We're told in 2 Peter 3:10 that there is coming a day when the heavens will pass away with a roar, and the heavenly bodies will be burned up and dissolved, and the earth and the works that are done on it will be exposed. There is going to be a new creation — a new heaven, a new earth, a New Jerusalem." Even as God spoke light into the first creation — God will have light in his second creation. For those who allowed the LIGHT of God expose their sin and then received the grace of Jesus who died and rose on their behalf — here is what we receive at the end.

Revelation 21:23-25 And the city has no need of sun or moon to shine on it, for the glory of God gives it light, and its lamp is the Lamb. By its light will the nations walk, and the kings of the earth will bring their glory into it, and its gates will never be shut by day—and there will be no night there. "The city" – that's the New Jerusalem," does not need the sun or the moon to shine on it for the glory of God gives its light and the lamb as it's lamp." THAT is what we — as men and women who have given our hearts to Jesus, the Light of the World, are going to walk into!

When Jesus came to this earth in His first coming — His glory was veiled in a tent of Humanity. But in that day we will see Christ face to face — and his glory will be completely unveiled for us! It is such glorious light that it will illuminate all of the new creation. There will be no darkness whatsoever. Sin is gone. Spiritual, Moral and Physical Darkness is gone.

Revelation 22:5 And night will be no more. They will need no light of lamp or sun, for the Lord God will be their light, and they will reign forever and ever. God's light permeates all of His new creation — and we become lamps through which His light shines to all of His new creation. And we reign with him. And there is no darkness in us. There is no darkness around us, nor will there ever be — forever and ever and ever. THAT is what we were MADE for! THAT is why we should hate the darkness — because it works against everything that we were created for. It works against the ultimate plan and purpose of God. We want to RESPOND now to the Word of God. We'll respond in giving — in communion — in song and in prayer. We'll respond by seeking to address the darkness within us — so that we can go out into the world — and the light of Christ can shine through us into the darkness that is out there. HUGE — The Christian life is a life defined by MOVEMENT. It begins with a man or woman moving away from darkness into the Light of Jesus. Then there is a movement back towards the world of darkness to share the light of the Gospel.

****

I wanted you all to know that I believe that Jesus is the Light of the World. No one can hold a candle to his everlasting light. But He has given us the power to hold our candle high to show others that we live in the light and not the darkness.

Both the Father and Jesus are the Good in the world and the Devil is the bad. Those that continually think of death and destruction are of the Devil and those that think of good are of God.

Islam is not good, no matter how many people describe them as "peaceful". Islam really describes a way of life from the moment you are born to the moment you die. They even describe what happens after you die.

Their leader is Mohammad who was a murderer, pedophile, adulterer, and many more descriptions and believed that by expanding Islam, the need to exterminate all infidels was important. An infidel is anyone that doesn't belong to the Islam belief.

Their believers have taken an oath to do this when ever the occasion arises. When they are small in numbers, they give the impression that they are peaceful and just want to "get along".

Once their numbers increase, they start to demand that their laws be included in the basic structure of the society in which they live. They, of course, will police their "own" and the community has nothing to fear.

Soon the need for their mosques is important to them and you are an segregationist, elitist or an infidel if you do not support their cause.

Once their cause is "supported" they start their obedience to their oath and by any means possible - including terrorism - they start their crusade. They have no regard to life and freedom and only the elimination of the infidels so that Islam may be increased.

In many countries around the world, Islam has grown exponentially and those countries aren't even aware of it, or are stricken with "dumbness" as to how to stop it. Those officials continue to over look the fact that Islam plays for keeps and nothing is going to stand in their way.

The very best way to overcome Islam is to shine a light on it. Our sure fire way of "exposing" Islam is to seek "The Light of the World" on it. Our God is the only guaranteed way of stopping Islam in its tracks. His light will shine so bright that Islam will remain in the dark where it will wither and die.

But God also gave us the ability to start the ball rolling. Along with His help, we can overcome the momentum that

Islam has generated and turn people away from the darkness and into the light.

How do we do that? So far I've talked about the one light that can save the world. That's a powerful light and one that can't be measured in lumens or foot candles, but one that can illuminate the New Jerusalem without the sun and where there will be no night.

We, as mortal beings, need to light one candle at a time and encourage others to do likewise. Once enough candles are lit, others will see the faults of Islam and turn against it's practices.

Stand Up for Jesus

Stand up, stand up for Jesus! ye soldiers of the cross;
Lift high His royal banner, it must not suffer loss:
From vict'ry unto vict'ry, His army shall He lead,
Till every foe is vanquished, and Christ is Lord indeed.
Stand up, stand up for Jesus! The trumpet call obey:
Forth to the mighty conflict, in this His glorious day;
Ye that are men now serve Him against unnumbered foes;
Let courage rise with danger, and strength to strength oppose.
Stand up, stand up for Jesus! Stand in His strength alone,
The arm of flesh will fail you, ye dare not trust your own;
Put on the gospel armor, and watching unto prayer,
Where calls the voice of duty, be never wanting there.
Stand up, stand up for Jesus! the strife will not be long;
This day the noise of battle, the next the victor's song;
To him that over cometh a crown of life shall be;
He with the King of glory shall reign eternally.

One Candle

For all those that have trouble believing that God is the Light of the World, I feel sorry for you - but - you still have a chance to be a good citizen. You need to take up your candle and hold it high so your friends clearly understand that you are in favor of changing the world to make it a better place to live.

One candle won't make a significant difference, but it takes the effort of one to get others started.

Take for example, the Tea Parties were formed just over a year or so ago and look at the difference they have made. They have already sent shivers up the spine of several liberals who have quit, decided not to run again or are just running scared.

**

All GOP Rivals 'Scare Me'
Senate Majority Leader Harry Reid dismissed talk that he would prefer to run

against tea party Republican Sharron Angle in November, saying all the top GOP
contenders could pose a threat.

Angle, a former state assemblywoman
who has been endorsed by the Tea Party
Express, squares off in the June 8 primary
against former state GOP Chairwoman
Sue Lowden and businessman Danny Tarkanian.

"I have no control over who's going to be
in the general election," Reid said at a
Memorial Day event in Boulder City, Nev.
"They all scare me."

But Lowden told Fox News' Neal Cavuto
that Reid is spending money from several
unions to back Angle because Reid polls
better against her.

And columnist Kathleen Parker wrote in
The Washington Post on Wednesday: "The
Senate majority leader figures he has a
better shot of keeping his seat in the fall if
Angle is his opponent instead of Sue Lowden. A recent Mason-Dixon Polling & Research survey shows Lowden holding a
three-point lead over Reid and Reid with
a three-point lead over Angle."

A poll by the Las Vegas Review-Journal
also showed Lowden and Tarkanian with
slight leads over Reid, and Reid with a

three-point edge over Angle. The paper stated that "Lowden has the best chance of defeating U.S. Sen. Harry Reid."

The Tea Party Express, which helped Scott Brown win his Senate seat in Massachusetts, has urged its estimated 350,000 national members to call Nevada voters on behalf of Angle.

"I have no idea who will be my opponent," Reid insisted. "I don't vote in the Republican primary so I don't study it very much."

****

Another email that shows how the Light of the Tea Parties is getting to the liberals:

**

What a unique way to look at things!

Written by a 82-year-old very wise lady. She gives us a whole new slant on the amazing job Obama is doing:

That is right - I will say it -- "THANK GOD FOR THE PRESIDENT."

1. He destroyed the Clinton Political Machine - driving a stake through the heart of Hillary's Presidential aspirations -something that no Republican was ever able to do. Remember when a Hillary Presidency scared the daylights out of you!

2. He killed off the Kennedy Dynasty - no more Kennedys trolling Washington looking for booze and women wanting rides home. American women and freedom are safer tonight!

3. He is destroying the Democratic Party before our eyes!

Dennis Moore had never lost a race - quit

Evan Bayh had never lost a race - quit

Byron Dorgan had never lost a race - quit

Harry Reid - soon to be GONE

These are just a handful of the Democrats whose political careers Obama has destroyed! By the end of 2010, dozens more will be gone.

In December of 2008, the Democrats were on the rise. In the last two election cycles, they had picked up 14 senate seats and 52 house seats. The press was touting the death of the Conservative Movement and the Republican Party. In just one year, Obama put a stop to all of this and will probably give the House, if not the Senate, back to the Republicans.

4. He has completely exposed liberals and progressives for what they are. Every generation seems to need to re-learn the lesson on why they should never actually put liberals in charge. He is bringing home the lesson very well.

Liberals tax, borrow, and spend - check

Liberals can't bring themselves to protect America - check

Liberals want to take over the economy - check

Liberals think they know what is best for everyone - check

Liberals aren't happy until they are running YOUR life - check

5. Obama has brought more Americans back to conservatism than anyone since Reagan. In one year, he has rejuvenated the conservative movement and brought out to the streets millions of freedom-loving Americans. Name one other time in your life when you saw your friends and neighbors this interested in taking back America!

6. His amazing leadership has sparked the greatest period of sales of firearms and ammunition this country has seen. Law-abiding citizens have rallied and have provided a "stimulus" to the sporting goods field while other industries have failed, faded or moved off-shore.

7. In all honesty, one year ago I was more afraid than I have been in my life. Not of the economy but of the direction our country was going. I thought Americans had forgotten what this country was all

about. My neighbors, friends and strangers proved to me that my lack of confidence of the greatness and wisdom of the American people was flat wrong.

8. When the American people wake up, no smooth-talking teleprompter reader can fool them!

Barack Obama is waking up America! Again, I want to say "Thank You Barack Obama! This is exactly the kind of change we desperately needed."

****

The Tea Party activities started in a very unique way. Read the following email and see how something can get started by one person and how quickly it can spread:

**

On February 19, 2009, in a broadcast from the floor of the Chicago Mercantile Exchange, CNBC Business News Network editor Rick Santelli loudly criticized the government plan to refinance mortgages, which had just been announced the day before, as "promoting bad behavior" by "subsidizing losers' mortgages" and raised the possibility of putting together a "Chicago Tea Party in July". A number of the traders and brokers around him cheered on his proposal, to the apparent amusement of the hosts in the studio. It was called "the rant heard round the world". According to The New Yorker writer Ben McGrath and New York Times reporter Kate Zernike, this is where the movement was first inspired to coalesce under the collective banner of "Tea Party." By the next day, guests on Fox News had already begun to mention this new "Tea Party."In response to Santelli, websites such as ChicagoTeaParty.com, registered in August 2008 by Chicago radio producer Zack Christenson, were live within twelve hours. About 10 hours after Santelli's remarks, re TeaParty.com was bought to coordinate Tea Parties scheduled for July 4, and as of March 4, was reported to be receiving 11,000 visitors a day.

According to The Huffington Post, a Facebook page was developed on February 20 calling for Tea Party protests across the country. Group administrators included Eric Odom of the conservative activist group FreedomWorks, and the group was created by Phil Kerpen from the conservative advocacy organization Americans for Prosperity -- the same group credited for the Denver "porkulus" protest as well as Mary Rakovich's early February 10 protest. Soon, the "Nationwide Chicago Tea Party" protest was coordinated across over 40 different cities for February 27, 2009, thus establishing the first national modern Tea Party protest.

****

Now tell me that one candle can't change things.

BO is NOT our president! He pretends to be, but he only represents the muslim side of the picture. We have a lot of traditions in this country and the Congress also has some. But, BO being who he is decided to change some of the most revered days this congress has. Please read the following:

**

Be Offended

In 1952, President Truman established one day a year as a National Day of Prayer.

In 1988, President Reagan designated the first Thursday in May of each year as the National Day of Prayer.

In June 2007, (then) Presidential candidate Barack Obama declared that the USA was no longer a Christian nation.

This year President Obama, canceled the 21st annual National Day of Prayer ceremony at the White House under the ruse of "not wanting to offend anyone".

On September 25, 2009 from 4 am until 7 PM, a National Day of Prayer for the Muslim religion was held on Capitol Hill, beside the White House. There were over 50,000 Muslims that day in DC.

I guess it doesn't matter if "Christians" are offended by this event - we obviously don't count as "anyone" anymore.

The direction this country is headed should strike fear in the heart of every Christian. Especially knowing that the Muslim religion believes that if Christians cannot be converted they should be annihilated.

This is not a rumor - Go to the web site to confirm this info:

www.islamoncapitolhill.com <http://www.islamoncapitolhill.com_/> (http://www.islamoncapitolhill.com/)

****

It's enough to make you sick. This president, who supposedly represents all of us, somehow has left all us Christians out in the cold. He apparently never learned that this country was founded on Christian principles and up until 2009 it has remained steady.

For any president to pledge his allegiance to Islam, while serving as our president, is mentally deficient and needs to be thrown out of office. Even his Democratic cronies are starting to bale out and getting some distance from him. I wouldn't be surprised that when the Senate and the House revert to conservative control (2010) BO will have to change his tune or be charged with "dereliction of duty", which is an impeachable offense.

You CAN NOT - I repeat - CAN NOT be a Islamic follower and be president of the USA. And - if he continues to play down the terror that Islam demonstrates almost daily, he is lying to himself as well as all of us. His hand picked a** kissers are good "YES" people and that's what he wants. There is nothing "presidential" about BO. He only fills the role of "king" and he will find that kings can be deposed.

We must all hold our candles high so that the rest of the country can rally around our cause.

Is this how HE will look when HE comes back for us?? !!!!!!! BEAUTIFUL!!!!
Isn't this the most awe inspiring picture
You've ever seen?

Twelve Candles

"Who were the twelve (12) disciples / apostles of Jesus Christ?"

Answer: The word "disciple" refers to a learner or follower. The word "apostle" means "one who is sent out." While Jesus was on earth, His twelve followers were called disciples. The twelve disciples followed Jesus Christ, learned from Him, and were trained by Him. After His resurrection and ascension, Jesus sent the disciples out to be His witnesses (Matthew 28:18-20; Acts 1:8). They were then referred to as the twelve apostles. However, even when Jesus was still on earth, the terms "disciples" and "apostles" were used somewhat interchangeably.

The original twelve disciples/apostles are listed in Matthew 10:2-4, "These are the names of the twelve apostles: first, Simon (who is called Peter) and his brother Andrew; James son of Zebedee, and his brother John; Philip and Bartholomew; Thomas and Matthew the tax collector; James son of Alphaeus, and Thaddaeus; Simon the Zealot and Judas Iscariot, who betrayed Him." The Bible also lists the twelve disciples/apostles in Mark 3:16-19 and Luke 6:13-16. A comparison of the three passages shows a couple of minor differences in the names. It seems that Thaddaeus was also known as "Judas, son of James" (Luke 6:16) and Lebbaeus (Matthew 10:3). Simon the Zealot was also known as Simon the Canaanite (Mark 3:18). Judas Iscariot, who betrayed Jesus, was replaced in the twelve apostles by Matthias (see Acts 1:20-26). Some Bible teachers view Matthias as an "invalid" apostle and believe that Paul was God's choice to replace Judas Iscariot as the twelfth apostle.

The twelve disciples/apostles were ordinary men whom God used in an extraordinary manner. Among the twelve were fishermen, a tax collector, and a revolutionary. The Gospels record the constant failings, struggles, and doubts of these twelve men who followed Jesus Christ. After witnessing Jesus' resurrection and ascension into heaven, the Holy Spirit transformed the disciples/apostles into powerful men of God who turned the world upside down (Acts 17:6). What was the change? The twelve apostles/disciples had "been with Jesus" (Acts 4:13). May the same be said of us!

The above information is available in your bibles and/or Google.

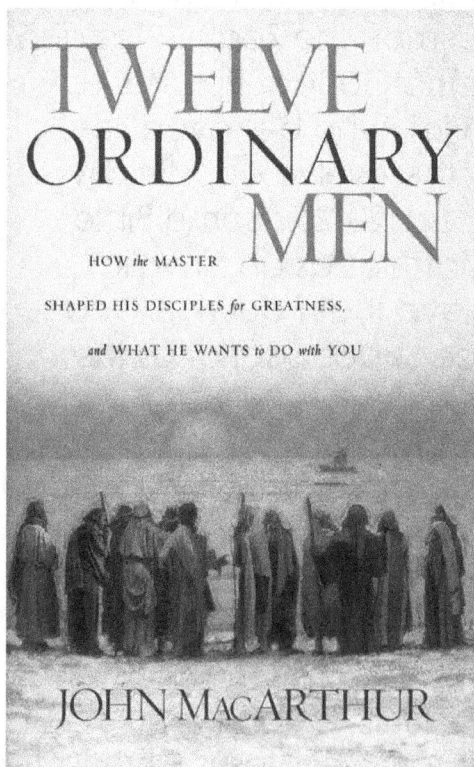

TWELVE
ORDINARY
MEN

HOW *the* MASTER

SHAPED HIS DISCIPLES *for* GREATNESS,

and WHAT HE WANTS *to* DO *with* YOU

JOHN MACARTHUR

Contrary to popular belief, we do not have to be perfect to do God's work. Look no further than the twelve disciples whose many weaknesses are forever preserved throughout the pages of the New Testament. Jesus chose ordinary men - fisherman, tax collectors, political zealots - and turned their weakness into strength, producing greatness from utter uselessness.

I used to listen to John MacArthur while driving to work every day. I enjoyed his radio sermons. I have not read his book, but am sure it is well worth reading.

Jesus turned twelve ordinary men into twelve candles to light the world. They all served Him well, except one, and spread the Good News all over the populated world. These men started with only the teaching from Jesus and ignited the Christian Faith. From one candle to twelve, the world was transformed and continues to this day.

Spreading the flame is the same as how a wild fire works. A small spark or flame ignites a larger flame and spreads. Although the fuel is burned, new grass and trees begin to grow and replenish what was there originally. We have to spread that flame so that new growth will begin. We barely have time left to get the fire going.

A new gallup poll has reviled that most Americans do not want BO for a second term. Although these numbers are satisfying, we cannot rest with just a majority. We should not be satisfied until one-hundred percent of the people feel the same way. This means that the fight must continue until the votes are counted. BO being from Chicago, there is no telling his plans for counting the votes.

The Islamics have a large toe-hold in the American government and they won't give it up easily. We must fight hard and long to overcome any possibility that their hold will never increase. If they don't mind blowing themselves up, or killing their children for the cause, or killing others, what would make you believe that we could win with just a majority?

This battle is not beyond the ability of our One Candle. The power of His light is sufficient to light even the darkest areas of the world. Even Mohammed can't hold a candle to Him.

However, we were not put on this earth just to wait to see what happens. We are His army and the General has given His orders.

Nearly 3,000 years ago the Hebrew prophets challenged the corruption of their political leaders. They held the kings accountable. When those in power broke the moral codes, the prophets stood and raised their voices in dissent.

We must also do the same. Raise you voice against the corruption that is infiltrating our government. Resist sending those representatives back to power that have allowed all this to happen. Send a message, loud and clear, to the remaining representatives that if they don't straighten up, they are next in line to be unemployed. The people MUST speak and change things before it is to late.

When I speak of being "to late". The example of Germany in the days of Hitler come to mind. Germany was enthralled with Adolf and only several years later found out that he had led them down the path of destruction. Hitler held his candle high and millions followed him believing he was leading the way to a better life.

Israel

Did President Obama Promise Saudi Arabia He Would Force Israel to Withdraw from Jerusalem?

I thought I couldn't be shocked by anything a politician did...but I was wrong! A stunning news report has just surfaced that President Obama has personally made a guarantee to King Abdullah of Saudi Arabia that he will force Israel to completely withdraw to the pre-1967 borders and promise a right of return to all Palestinians which will allow them to return to Israel.

According to the report, "Diplomatic sources said Obama relayed a pledge to Saudi King Abdullah that he would take any measure to ensure an Israeli withdrawal from the West Bank and Jerusalem over the next 18 months. They said Obama relayed the pledge to Abdullah during the president's trip to Riyadh in June 2009, about four months after he assumed office, in exchange for Abdullah's help in arranging the end of the Taliban war in Afghanistan."

These same sources believe that President Obama reiterated his pledge to King Abdullah at their meeting two weeks ago at the White House.

"Obama believes the Saudis are the most important element in his strategy to withdraw from Afghanistan," a diplomatic source familiar with the Obama-Abdullah talks said. "Abdullah said he was ready to talk to Taliban, but asked for a clear and definitive promise to deliver Israel."

This promise represents an outrageous betrayal of America's best friend and ally in the Middle East. The clear implication is that President Obama is willing to trade Israel's security...and even Israel's survival...for the sake of ending the fighting in Afghanistan to gain a political advantage. The President has been putting on a show for mid-term political purposes to convince American Jews and pro-Israel Christians that he is Israel's best friend...but this story reveals a very different reality.

I am writing you today because you are a friend of Israel and I know you agree with me that we must support Israel at this crisis moment. Will you speak out and say that the President does not speak for you when he attacks the very future of Israel? Will you send your support to the Jewish people so that they know they are not alone? Will you stand for Israel in its moment of crisis and great need?

It has long been an open secret that many members of the State Department, including special envoy Richard Holbrooke, are virulently anti-Israel. In fact the report states that Holbrooke was the one who made the original commitment to King Abdullah that America would force Israel to agree to Saudi Arabia's "peace plan" in exchange for help from Saudi Arabia in dealing with the Taliban in Afghanistan who receive significant funding from Saudi Arabia.

That tangled relationship where our supposed ally Saudi Arabia is providing money to the terrorist Taliban fighters who are killing our soldiers and Marines in Afghanistan highlights the folly of turning against Israel. And make no mistake about it, the Saudi Arabian plan that the President has promised to pursue is a death sentence for Israel.

The pre-1967 borders are completely indefensible and the "right of return" would destroy Israel's very nature as a Jewish state. The President's foolish promise places America in direct opposition to the prophecies and promises of the Word of God...and places us in danger of receiving the curse God pronounced in Genesis

12:1-3 on all those who harm the descendants of Abraham.

The Jerusalem Prayer Team needs your help to get this stunning news out. The Saudi Arabian government has major financial stakes in the American media, and they are not eager for this news to spread. Please forward this email to everyone on your list and ask them to join in raising our voices in defense of Israel.

We cannot turn our backs on Israel at this crisis moment. The threat it faces from Iran's nuclear program is literally a matter of life and death for tens of thousands...and if America deserts Israel, the consequences to the world will be dire indeed. Please join me in praying urgently that God will confound the plans and schemes of those who hate the Chosen People and that He will bless His people with peace.

Your Ambassador to Jerusalem,
Dr. Michael Evans

****

Israel is our first line of defense. If Israel should fall, the entire Middle East will be gunning for the UK and the USA. We will be the last bastion of freedom left in the world. Sure there are other countries that have "freedom", but the United States is the last "power" that has it.

Israel is surrounded by enemies that would gather together, when they thought they could, and start another war. Israel has already fought three wars since it's inception on May 14,1948 and several others that could have led to outright war.

Their war of Independence started just one day after they became a nation. The Arab states just couldn't stand to have Jews living next to them.

The Arabs tried war again on June 5, 1967 which lasted only six days. Israel jumped out first and then completely annihilated the Arab coalition.

The Arabs again tried war with a surprise attack on Yom Kippur, October 6, 1973. Although Israel was caught unaware they quickly overcame the surprise and rallied to crush the Arabs again.

A peace treaty with Egypt was signed in 1979, the one plus that came out of the Carter administration. A peace treaty with Jordan was signed in 1994.

Israel has had several small wars with Lebanon and other factions in between, but not on the scale of the three major wars. During the first Gulf war, Israel was targeted by Iraq with scud missiles, but was defended by the US with our own "scud busters". Israel also "took-out" a nuclear site in Iraq and prevented them from building weapons of mass destruction. Israel is not a country to be messed with and we would do ourselves a giant favor to help them in every way possible.

Why am I bringing this all up now? Because our president, BO is a Muslim and you find that Israel is surrounded by them. Read the following:

**

Why doesn't Michelle travel with Barack to Arab countries? I found this and just thought I'd pass it along;

By: Attorney John W. King

If you check Obama's last trip overseas, his wife left just after their visit to France as stated below. She has yet to accompany him to any Arab country. Think about it. This was sent to me from a very good and reliable friend. The pieces of the puzzle just keep on coming together! Interesting...

Travel for Obama;
I was at Blockbusters renting videos, and as I was going along the wall, there was a video called "Obama." There were two men next to me. We talked about Obama. These guys were Arabs and I asked them why they thought Michele Obama headed home following her visit in France instead of traveling on to Saudi Arabia and Turkey with her husband. They told me she couldn't go to Saudi Arabia , Turkey or Iraq . I said "Laura Bush went to Saudi Arabia, Turkey and Dubai." They said that Obama is a Muslim, and by Muslim law he would not be allowed to bring his wife into countries that accept shari'ah law. I just thought it was interesting that two Arabs at Blockbusters accept the idea that we're being led by a Muslim who follows the Islamic creed. They al-

so said that's the reason he bowed to the King of Saudi Arabia. It was a signal to the Muslim world. Just thought you would like to know.

When I received this it made sense to me, but there were also a couple blank spots. Thus, I sent it to a friend who is a Middle Eastern Scholar and expert, Dr. Jim Murk. Here is his explanation that states a little clearer what the Arabs at Blockbuster were saying.

"An orthodox Muslim man would never take his wife on a politically oriented trip to any nation which practices shari'ah law, which includes Saudi Arabia .. This is true and it is why Obama left Michelle in Europe or at home when he went to especially Arab countries. He knows Muslim protocol; this included his bowing to the Saudi king. Obama is regarded as a Muslim in these countries simply because he was born to a Muslim father. Under Muslim law, once you are a Muslim, you are always considered a Muslim.
Note that he has downplayed his Christianity -- even spoke of his Muslim faith with

George Stephanopoulos -- by not publicly joining a Christian church in D.C., but simply attending the chapel or services at Camp David . He also played down the fact that the USA was a Christian country and said, unbelievably, that it was one of the largest Muslim nations in the world, which is nonsense. He has also publicly taken the part of the Palestinians in the conflict with Israel . Finally he ignored the National Day of Prayer. He is bad news. He is God's judgment on America .."

-- Jim Murk

Thus once again ACTIONS do speak louder than words. Check out the Obama's. Do they appear treasonous to you or is it just millions of us who think so?

God help us!

Have you wondered why Barack Hussein Obama has insisted that the U.S. Attorney General hold the trials for the 911 Murdering Muslims Terrorists in Civilian Courts as Common Criminals instead of as Terrorists who attacked the United States of America ?

Think about this: If the Muslim Terrorists are tried in Military Tribunals, convicted, and sentenced to DEATH by the Military Tribunal, BY LAW of the United States , Barack Hussein Obama, as President of the United States , would be required to SIGN their Death Warrants before they could be EXECUTED. He would not be required to sign the death warrants if sentenced to death by a Civilian Court .

Think about the Muslim Jihadist, Major Hassan who slaughtered his fellow soldiers at Ft. Hood, Texas . Major Hassan did not want to go to Afghanistan and be a part of anything that could lead to the deaths of fellow Muslims. He stated that Muslims could not and should not KILL FELLOW MUSLIMS.

Is the motive for Barack Hussein Obama's decision to make sure he doesn't have to sign the death warrants for the Muslim Terrorists? Why would he, as President of the United States, not want to sign the death warrants for Muslim Terrorists who attacked the United States and MURDERED over 3,000 innocent United States Citizens on 9/11? Could it be that he is FORBIDDEN BY HIS RELIGION to have anything to do with the execution of Muslims? (this still doesn't explain the stoning of Muslim women by other Muslims- Ox)

Think about that! Join me in opening our ears, eyes and minds to what THEIR President is doing. PLEASE pass this along to your friends if you agree that this sounds reasonable.

John W. King, Attorney at Law

****

Non-Christians find it hard to believe we are living in the last days of earth's history. It's in the Bible, II Peter 3:3-4, TLB. "First, I want to remind you that in the last days there will come scoffers who will do every wrong they can think of, and laugh at the truth. This will be their line of argument: 'So Jesus promised to come back, did He? Then where is He? He'll never come! Why, as far back as anyone can remember everything has remained exactly as it was since the first day of creation.'"

The coming of the Antichrist is a sign of the end. It's in the Bible, I John 2:18, TLB. "Dear children, this world's last hour has come. You have heard about the Antichrist who is coming—the one who is against Christ—and already many such persons have appeared. This makes us all the more certain that the end of the world is near."

Did Jesus say when the end would come? It's in the Bible, Matthew 24:14, NIV. "And this gospel of the kingdom will be preached in the whole world as a testimony to all nations, and then the end will come."

Men posing as Jesus will try to deceive people in the last days. It's in the Bible, Matthew 24:23-24, NIV. "At that time if anyone says to you, 'Look, here is the Christ! or 'There He is! do not believe it. For false Christ's and false prophets will appear and perform great signs and miracles to deceive even the elect—if that were possible."

There will be signs in the sun, moon, and stars. It's in the Bible, Matthew 24:29-30, NIV. "Immediately after the distress of those days the sun will be darkened, and the moon will not give its light; the stars will fall from the sky, and the heavenly bodies will be shaken. At that time the sign of the

Son of Man will appear in the sky, and all the nations of the earth will mourn. They will see the Son of Man coming on the clouds of the sky, with power and great glory."

What moral conditions will be characteristic of society in the last days? It's in the Bible, II Timothy 3:1-5, NIV. "But mark this: There will be terrible times in the last days. People will be lovers of themselves, lovers of money, boastful, proud, abusive, disobedient to their parents, ungrateful, unholy, without love, unforgiving, slanderous, without self-control, brutal, not lovers of the good, treacherous, rash, conceited, lovers of pleasure rather than lovers of God—having a form of godliness but denying its power. Have nothing to do with them."

An increase in knowledge and travel is a sign of the last days. It's in the Bible, Daniel 12:4, TLB. "But Daniel, keep this prophecy a secret; seal it up so that it will not be understood until the end times, when travel and education shall be vastly increased!"

What other signs of the last days does the Bible mention? It's in the Bible, Luke 21:25-26, NIV. "There will be signs in the sun, moon, and stars. On the earth, nations will be in anguish and perplexity at the roaring and tossing of the sea. Men will faint from terror, apprehensive of what is coming on the world, for the heavenly bodies will be shaken."

Talk of peace and safety are a sign of the last days. It's in the Bible, I Thessalonians 5:2-3, NIV. "For you know very well that the day of the Lord will come like a thief in the night. While people are saying, 'Peace and safety,' destruction will come on them suddenly, as labor pains on a pregnant woman, and they will not escape."

What are people to do when they see these things taking place? It's in the Bible, Matthew 24:42-44, TLB. "So be prepared, for you don't know what day your Lord is coming. Just as a man can prevent trouble from thieves by keeping watch for them, so you can avoid trouble by always being ready for My unannounced return."

Israel is the only Middle Eastern country that has contributed anything, of a substantial nature, for the beneficial use of mankind. The only thing the Muslim countries have contributed are hate and killing. If they are so keen on becoming a better place to live they wouldn't put up with all the wrongs their fellow followers are committing.

Israel is the candle that is burning brightly in this hot bed of hate. We need to make sure their candle doesn't go out.

**

From the desk of Paul Belien 06-24-2010-

"Decoy Jew" is a new phrase in the Netherlands . Jews are no longer safe in major Dutch cities such as Amsterdam. Since 1999, Jewish organizations in the Netherlands have been complaining that Jews who walk the Dutch streets wearing skullcaps risk verbal and physical attacks by young Muslims. Being insulted, spat at or attacked are some of the risks associated with being recognizable as a Jew in contemporary Western Europe.

Last week, a television broadcast showed how three Jews with skullcaps, two adolescents and an adult, were harassed within thirty minutes of being out in the streets of Amsterdam. Young Muslims spat at them, mocked them, shouted insults and made Nazi salutes. "Dirty Jew, go back to your own country," a group of Moroccan youths shouted at a young indigenous Dutch Jew. "It is rather ironic," the young man commented, adding that if one goes out in a burka one encounters less hostility than if one wears a skullcap.

In an effort to arrest the culprits who terrorize Jews, the Amsterdam authorities have ordered police officers to walk the streets disguised as Jews. The Dutch police already disguise officers as "decoy prostitutes, decoy gays and decoy grannies" to deter muggings and attacks on prostitutes, homosexuals and the elderly. Apparently sending out the decoys has helped reduce street crime. The "decoy Jew" has now been added to the police attributes.

The deployment of "decoy Jews", however, is being criticized by leftist parties such as the Dutch Greens. Evelien van Roemburg, an Amsterdam counselor of the Green Left Party, says that using a decoy by the police amounts to provoking a crime, which is itself a criminal offense under Dutch law.

Unfortunately, the situation in Amsterdam is not unique. Jews in other Dutch cities also regularly complain about harassment. So do Jews in neighboring countries.

On Monday, the Belgian newspaper De Standaard reported that large numbers of Jews are leaving Antwerp for America, Britain or Israel . Antwerp - nicknamed the "Jerusalem of the North" - is one of the major centers of Jewish culture in the Low Countries. "In London, you are not harassed if you wear a skullcap, but here you are," a young Antwerp Jew told the paper.

Kleinblatt, a famous Jewish Antwerp bakery, which has been handed down from father to son since 1903, will soon break with that tradition because the baker's son has emigrated to the U.S. "We no longer feel safe and welcome here," a young Jew who is leaving for London told De Standaard. "Muslim immigrants blame us for what is happening in Israel ." Another young Jew, who is leaving for New York, says: "New York is a paradise for Jews. Unlike Belgium, non-Jews in America are pro-Israel."

Ultra-orthodox Jews remain in Antwerp , but the less orthodox are leaving in droves. Even Jacques Wenger, the director of Shomre Hadas, the Jewish community center in Antwerp, is emigrating to Israel. If the current trend continues, he predicts, in fifty years' time there will be no Jews left in Antwerp except for the ultra-orthodox.

It is often said that the Jews are the canary in the coal mine. When the Jews feel compelled to leave, the light of freedom is being extinguished. Something is badly wrong when the police need to deploy "decoy Jews." Once again, the specter of anti-Semitism is haunting Europe. If the Europeans do not stand with the Jews, they deserve no freedom themselves and cities such as Amsterdam and Antwerp will soon be Islamic cities.

****

History does repeat itself. If we don't pay attention to it, history will rule our lives. History is meant to be a learning curve that we don't repeat the same mistakes we've made in the past. However, most people don't like reading about history or believe they can change it this time around. One of the problems that we suffer from is just plain old "common sense". Here is an article from London about the very same:

**

An Obituary printed in the London Times --- NOT a joke .... and it really makes you think!

Today we mourn the passing of a beloved old friend, Common Sense, who has been with us for many years. No one knows for sure how old he was, since his birth records were long ago lost in bureaucratic red tape.

He will be remembered as having cultivated such valuable lessons as:

- Knowing when to come in out of the rain;

- Why the early bird gets the worm;

- Life isn't always fair;

- and maybe it was my fault.

Common Sense lived by simple, sound financial policies (don't spend more than you can earn) and reliable strategies (adults, not children, are in charge).

His health began to deteriorate rapidly when well-intentioned but overbearing regulations were set in place: Reports of a 6-year-old boy charged with sexual harassment for kissing a classmate; teens suspended from school for using mouthwash after lunch; and a teacher fired for reprimanding an unruly student, only worsened his condition.

Common Sense lost ground when parents attacked teachers for doing the job that they themselves had failed to do in disciplining their unruly children.

It declined even further when schools were required to get parental consent to administer sunscreen or an Aspirin to a student; but could not inform parents when a student became pregnant and wanted to have an abortion.

Common Sense took a beating when you couldn't defend yourself from a burglar in your own home and the burglar could sue you for assault..

Common Sense lost the will to live as the churches became businesses; and criminals received better treatment than their victims.

Common Sense finally gave up the will to live, after a woman failed to realize that a steaming cup of coffee was hot. She spilled a little in her lap, and was promptly awarded a huge settlement.

Common Sense was preceded in death

- by his parents, Truth and Trust;

- by his wife, Discretion;

- by his daughter, Responsibility and

- by his son, Reason.

He is survived by his 4 stepbrothers:

- I Know My Rights

- I Want It Now

- Someone Else Is To Blame

- I am a Victim

Not many attended his funeral because so few realized he was gone.

REMEMBER, GROWING OLDER IS MANDATORY. GROWING UP IS OPTIONAL

IMMIGRATION

So much is being discussed today about should all the "illegals" be granted amnesty or not. The majority of the country say they should only gain access to the United States the same way as the older generation of immigrants did. Gain a sponsor, have a place to live, find a job, pay your taxes, etc, etc. What ever the number of illegals that are here today, most EXPECT free lunches, healthcare, subsidies, no taxes, preferential treatment and the right to be given citizenship.

Most Mexican women, as well as other countries, race across the border just to have their babies. Those babies automatically become citizens just because they were born here. Plus they get FREE hospital care as well as social assistance.

These women pop out babies left and right and soon the population has expanded to the point that can't be controlled. More and more of these poor, abused, downtrodden people from south of the border are filling our hospitals, jails, welfare offices and jobs. The old argument that they only take the jobs white folk don't want doesn't hold water. They're so used to working for 50 cents and hour so when they are offered a dollar and hour it's a huge raise. However you can't live on a dollar an hour so the government steps in to make a difference. As BO sees it - these are his kind of votes.

**

What if 20 Million Illegal Aliens Vacated America?

I, Tina Griego, journalist for the Denver Rocky Mountain News, wrote a column titled, "Mexican Visitor's Lament"- 10/25/07.

I interviewed Mexican journalist Evangelina Hernandez while visiting Denver last week. Hernandez said, "Illegal aliens pay rent, buy groceries, buy clothes. What Happens to your country's economy if 20 million people go away?" Hummm, I thought, what would happen, so I did my due diligence, buried my nose as a reporter into the FACTS I found below.

It's a good question; it deserves an honest answer.

Over 80% of Americans demand secured borders and illegal migration stopped. But what would happen if all 20 million or more vacated America? The answers I found may surprise you!

In California, if 3.5 million illegal aliens moved back to Mexico, it would leave an extra $10.2 billion to spend on overloaded school systems, bankrupt hospitals and overrun prisons. It would leave highways cleaner, safer and less congested. Everyone could understand one another as English became the dominant language again.

In Colorado, 500,000 illegal migrants, plus their 300,000 kids and grandchildren would move back home, mostly to Mexico. That would save Coloradans an estimated $2 billion (other experts say $7 billion) annually in taxes that pay for schooling, medical, social services and in-carceration costs. It means 12,000 gang members would vanish out of Denver a-lone.

Colorado would save more than $20 million in prison costs, and the terror that those 7,300 alien criminals set upon local citizens. Denver Officer Don Young and hundreds of Colorado victims would not have suffered death, accidents, rapes and other crimes by illegal's.

Denver Public Schools would not suffer a 67% drop-out/flunk-out rate because of thousands of illegal alien students speaking 41 different languages. At least 200,000 vehicles would vanish from our grid locked cities in Colorado. Denver's 4% unemployment rate would vanish as our working poor would gain jobs at a living wage.

In Florida, 1.5 million illegal's would return the Sunshine State back to America, the rule of law and English.

In Chicago, Illinois, 2.1 million illegal's would free up hospitals, schools, prisons and highways for a safer, cleaner and more crime-free experience.

If 20 million illegal aliens returned home, the U.S. Economy would return to the rule of law. Employers would hire legal American citizens at a living wage. Everyone would pay their fair share of taxes because they wouldn't be working off the books. That would result in an additional $401 Billion in IRS income taxes collected annually, and an equal amount for local, state and city coffers.

No more push1 for Spanish or 2 for English. No more confusion in American schools that now must contend with over 100 languages that degrade the educational system for American kids. Our overcrowded schools would lose more than two million illegal alien kids at a cost of billions in ESL and free breakfasts and lunches.

We would lose 500,000 illegal criminal alien inmates at a cost of more than $1.6 billion annually. That includes 15,000 MS-13 gang members who distribute $130 billion in drugs annually and would vacate our country.

In cities like L. A., 20,000 members of the 18th Street Gang would vanish from our nation. No more Mexican forgery gangs for ID theft from Americans!

Losing more than 20 million people would clear up some of our crowded highways and gridlock. Cleaner air and less drinking and driving American deaths by illegal aliens!

America's economy is drained. Taxpayers are harmed. Employers get rich. Over $80 billion annually wouldn't return to the aliens' home countries by cash transfers. Illegal migrants earned half that money untaxed, which further drains America's economy which currently suffers an $8.7 trillion debt. $8.7 trillion debt!

At least 400,000 anchor babies would not be born in our country, costing us $109 billion per year per cycle. At least 86 hospitals in California, Georgia, and Florida would still be operating instead of being bankrupt out of existence because illegal's pay nothing via the EMTOLA Act.

Americans wouldn't suffer thousands of TB and hepatitis cases rampant in our country - brought in by illegal's unscreened at our borders.

Our cities would see 20 million less people driving, polluting and grid locking our cities. It would also put the progressives on the horns of a dilemma; illegal aliens and their families cause 11% of our greenhouse gases.

Over one million of Mexico's poorest citizens now live inside and along our border from Brownsville, Texas, to San Diego, California, in what the New York Times called, colonias or new neighborhoods. Trouble is, those living areas resemble Bom - bay and Calcutta where grinding poverty, filth, diseases, drugs, crimes, poor sanitation and worse.

The New York Times reported them to be America's new Third World inside our own country. Within 20 years, at their current growth rate, they expect 20 million residents of those colonias. (I've seen them personally in Texas and Arizona; it's sickening beyond anything you can imagine.)

By enforcing our laws, we could repatriate them back to Mexico. We should invite 20 million aliens to go home, fix their own countries and/or make a better life in Mexico. We already invite a million people into our country legally, more than all other countries combined annually. We cannot and must not allow anarchy at our borders, more anarchy within our borders and growing lawlessness at every level in our nation.

It's time to stand up for our country, our culture, our civilization and our way of life.

Interesting Statistics!

Here are 14 reasons illegal aliens should vacate America, and I hope they are forwarded over and over again until they are read so many times that the reader gets sick of reading them:

1. $14 billion to $22 billion dollars are spent each year on welfare to illegal ali-

ens (that,s Billion with a B). http://tinyurl..com/zob77

2. $2.2 billion dollars are spent each year on food assistance programs such as food stamps, WIC, and free school lunches for illegal aliens.
http://www.cis.org/articles/2004/fiscalexec.html

3. $7.5 billion dollars are spent each year on Medicaid for illegal aliens. http://www.cis.org/articles/2004/fiscalexec.html

4. $12 billion dollars are spent each year on primary and secondary school education for children here illegally and they still cannot speak a word of English. http://transcripts.cnn.com/TRANSCRIPTS/0604/01/ldt.01.html

5. $27 billion dollars are spent each year for education for the American-born children of illegal aliens, known as anchor babies. http://transcripts.cnn.com/TRANSCRIPTS/0604/01/ldt.01.html

6. $3 Million Dollars PER DAY is spent to incarcerate illegal aliens. That's $1.2 Billion a

a-year. http://transcripts.cnn.com/TRAN
SCRIPTS/0604/01/ldt.01.html

7. 28% percent of all federal prison in-mates are illegal aliens.
http://transcripts.cnn.com/TRANSCRIPTS/0
604/01/ldt.01.html

8. $190 billion dollars are spent each year on illegal aliens for welfare and social services by the American taxpayers.
 http://transcripts.cnn.com/TRANSCRIPTS/0
610/29/ldt.01.html

9. $200 billion dollars per year in sup-pressed American wages are caused by the illegal aliens.
 http://transcripts.cnn.com/TRANSCRIPTS/0
604/01/ldt.01.html

10. The illegal aliens in the United States have a crime rate that's two and a half times that of white non-illegal aliens. In particular, their children, are going to

make a huge additional crime problem in the U.S.
http://transcripts.cnn.com/TRANSCRIPTS/0606/12/ldt.01.html

11. During the year 2005, there were 8 to 10 MILLION illegal aliens that crossed our southern border with as many as 19,500 illegal aliens from other terrorist countries. Over 10,000 of those were middle-eastern terrorists. Millions of pounds of drugs, cocaine, meth, heroine, crack,guns, and marijuana crossed into the U.S.from the southern border.
http://tinyurl.com/t9sht

12. The National Policy Institute, estimates that the total cost of mass deportation would be between $206 and $230 billion, or an average cost of between $41and $46 billion annually over a five-year period.
http://www.nationalpolicyinstitute./.org/publications.php?b=deportation

13. In 2006, illegal aliens sent home $65 BILLION in remittances back to their countries of origin, to their families and friends.
http://www.rense.com/general75/niht.htm

14. The dark side of illegal immigration: Nearly one million sex crimes are committed by illegal immigrants in the United States!
http://www.drdsk.com/articleshtml

Total cost: A whopping $538.3 BILLION DOLLARS A YEAR!

****

That's about $1,800.00 from each man, woman and child just to pay for these illegals.

**

This email is directed to those of you who attend Christian churches.

Once again today, a group of national Christian leaders testified before Congress that the Christian thing to do about immigration during this time of high unemployment is

a) to give permanent work permits to illegal aliens

b) and to import more foreign workers.

Below is the testimony of the sole Christian layman who was a witness among the clergy. I think you will agree that his theological understanding is far more perceptive than that of the Catholic, Baptist and Evangelical clergy who insisted on rewarding millions of illegal aliens.

Dr. James Edwards' key point was this:

MANY NATIONAL CHRISTIAN LEADERS LOBBY FOR MERCY (AMNESTY) FOR ILLEGAL ALIENS BUT THAT MERCY WOULD CREATE INJUSTICE FOR INNOCENT LAW-ABIDING AMERICANS (ESPECIALLY THE UNEMPLOYED) GOVERNMENTS ARE CALLED TO PROVIDE JUSTICE

I have some hope that most of the nation's clergy will be reluctant to join the many national Methodist, Lutheran, Episcopal, Assemblies of God, Presbyterian and Baptist leaders in their lobbying for amnesty.

But most of your pastors probably have never heard anything but a sentimentalist appeal for amnesty based on Christian and Jewish scripture's admonition to not mistreat the alien (or sojourner, or stranger).

You owe it to your pastor to ask him/her to read Dr. Edwards' testimony before perhaps following good intentions that lead to extremely unpopular and theologically questionable pronouncements in favor of amnesty and "comprehensive immigration reform."

We invite all clergy to join the clergy already among our more than 1 million members in reviewing the content of our website at www.NumbersUSA.com. NumbersUSA has always called for the humane treatment of illegal aliens and works for reduced overall immigration based on the numbers but not the character or characteristics of immigrants.

AN ETHICAL CHRISTIAN APPROACH TO IMMIGRATION REFORM

by Dr. James Edwards

Madame Chairman, Ranking Member King, and distinguished members of the subcommittee, thank you for inviting me to appear before you today. It is right to consider how Scripture and Judeo-Christian principles should inform such public issues as immigration. I appreciate the opportunity to share my own considered views on this subject.

The critical point to begin from is to differentiate between what the Bible teaches are moral imperatives applicable to individuals and those that are applicable corporately.

That is, some precepts might bind one as a Christian that do not apply to the United States government. Indeed, biblical precepts in which Christ requires us personally to show mercy or compassion or forgiveness might not apply to the civil government of the nation-state of which we are citizens. Sometimes, such application would actually be harmful and wrong.

First, I will discuss a key biblical principle that relates to today's American immigration debate. Second, I will suggest some implications of "comprehensive immigration reform" that ought to inform Congress's immigration policymaking.

To begin, what are the most relevant principles from Scripture that relate to U.S. immigration policy in 2010? I have written about this at length elsewhere and testified before this subcommittee on the subject.

So, I will focus this morning on one key principle.

Christians as individuals are bound to a high moral imperative, which should be familiar to many of us: Love the Lord with all your heart, soul, strength, and mind, and love your neighbor as yourself. These cornerstone precepts, as elaborated by Jesus in the Sermon on the Mount and elsewhere in the Bible, instruct believers to go so far as to "love your enemies," "bless those who curse you," and care for "the least of these my brothers." Considered alongside Micah 6:8 — "He has showed you, O man, what is good. And what does the Lord require of you? To act justly and to love mercy and to walk humbly with your God." — it becomes clear that faithfully living up to those standards is tough. In fact, it is impossible even for those indwelt by the Holy Spirit. In other words, exhibiting Christian mercy and compassion is not for sissies.

But do these high standards apply to civil government? To an extent. For instance, U.S. laws reflect such biblical standards as providing for due process, impartial justice, and prohibiting torturous punishment of criminals. But to attempt to require civil authority to display the same manner of mercy or compassion that individual Christians are commanded to display would be ludicrous. Yet that is what certain advocates in the immigration debate unreasonably demand.

We must understand the God-given role of civil government. Romans 13 clearly teaches that civil authorities are God's agents in their own specific jurisdictions to constrain evil. Civil authority wields the sword of justice to protect the innocent within its jurisdiction and to punish law-breakers. The mission, described here and in I Peter 2 and Titus 3, is to "carry out God's wrath on the wrongdoer." In the Bible, the "things that are Caesar's" are concentrated on justice. God deputizes civil authorities as part of His common grace, because we live in a fallen world. Evil exists, and government constrains evil within a body politic.

A civil government necessarily and prudently refrains from overdoing compassion or mercy. The reasons include that officials act merely as agents of the citizens they represent. Public acts of government differ fundamentally from individual acts. Grasping this concept is critical. Otherwise, it could lead to misguided and erroneous courses of action, such as jumping from the early church members' voluntarily sharing their private resources within the body of believers in Acts 2 to conjuring some supposed biblical directive for socialism.

Compassion and mercy, as exercised by an individual, amount to his or her deciding willingly to bear an injustice. It is merciful when a private person turns the other cheek, goes the extra mile, gives up his tunic, and shares with a beggar. However, the government cannot itself do any of those things. Rather, the government only can obligate the members of its society and their common resources.

Thus,

A compassionate act often becomes an injustice when compelled by civil government.

Trying to codify mercy, the agents who are supposed to be the guardians of justice for their citizens can end up imposing injustice upon the innocent.

What might constitute an act of mercy when an individual does it becomes an injustice against the members of the body politic when government employs its sword of "justice" to compel such "mercy." This amounts to a grotesque misuse of power. Even if well intended, such government action is actually unjust.

So how does this discussion apply to our present immigration debate? It is advisable to consider the impact of proposed "comprehensive immigration reform" on our fellow Americans. More than the welfare of illegal immigrants is at stake here.

And the foremost obligation, legally and morally, of the U.S. government is the welfare of American citizens.

The American people too often end up being the forgotten victims of "comprehensive immigration reform." That is certainly the case were the CIR ASAP Act or the Schumer-Reid-Graham proposal to be enacted. The goals of those bills are principally granting legal status to nearly all of the estimated 11 million unlawful alien residents, as well as guaranteeing a flood of job competition from foreign workers every year for the foreseeable future.

The supposed penalties such schemes would impose on illegal aliens amount to what the law currently would require: payment of certain fees, undergo a background check, and some modest step toward English acquisition. These sanctions hardly constitute meaningful penalty or punishment.

Plainly, the government's display of "mercy" toward millions of people who willfully broke this nation's laws forces its own innocent citizens to stomach substantial injustice.

Who would "comprehensive immigration reform" hurt?

It would put the most vulnerable Americans at risk — native-born minorities,

Americans with no more than a high school education including dropouts,

legal immigrants, our teenagers trying to land that first rung on the career ladder, veterans, the disabled, and convicts seeking to amend their lives in society.

Before the recession started, native-born youth and those with less education were experiencing extra high unemployment — 11.6 percent for dropouts and 10.6 percent for those with only a high school diploma in the third quarter 2007.

Needless to say, their joblessness has worsened. Some 21 million unemployed or underemployed native-born Americans lacked a job or were discouraged from looking for work in the third quarter 2009.

"Comprehensive immigration reform" would exacerbate their economic prospects, both by adding many more job competitors to the U.S. labor pool and depressing the wages that U.S. workers could otherwise command. This policy amounts to substituting labor for capital, which runs directly counter to the "American system of manufacture," based on a tighter labor market and led to the development of a strong middle class.

Today, fewer than half of American teens are in the labor force, compared with two-thirds in 1994. Adding more foreign workers who have displaced our teenagers from job opportunities accounts for a large share of this situation. The one-two punch of amnesty and massively more "guest workers" would further kill summer job opportunities for our teens.

The impact of legalizing the 7-8 million illegal aliens in the U.S. workforce and the 11 million total estimated unlawfully resident aliens, plus the untold thousands of foreign workers brought in under the proposed "guest worker" program (lopped on top of the several existing guest worker visa programs) would force Americans who face the toughest job-search circumstances into head-to-head job competition with unimaginable numbers of foreign competitors.

It would also drive down their wages. Already, immigration of the scale we have had in recent decades negatively affects

U.S. natives' wages. Scholarly analysis bears this out. For example, Harvard economist George Borjas has attributed immigration with directly reducing yearly average native-born men's wages by 4 percent, or $1,700, between 1980 and 2000. For native dropouts, immigration's wage depression was 7.4 percent over the same period. Northeastern University scholars found nearly all the U.S. job growth from 2000 to 2004 was filled by immigrant workers.

Consider in detail vulnerable Americans' employment situation, which was already bleak as of third quarter 2009. I am citing the U-6 unemployment figure, which counts those actively looking but without a job, the underemployed, and people who have stopped looking for full-time employment. U-6 unemployment for native-born high school dropouts: 32.4 percent. U-6 unemployment for native-born blacks 18-29 years old with a high school diploma only: 39.8 percent. U-6 unemployment for native-born blacks who dropped out of school: 42.2 percent. U-6 unemployment for native-born Latinos without a high school diploma: 35.6 percent. U-6 unemployment for native-born Latinos 18-29 years old with only a diploma: 33.9 percent.

We do not have a labor shortage. Further, the wages of the least educated and less skilled fellow Americans have been declining for decades, beginning well before the current recession. Male high school dropouts have seen hourly wages fall 22 percent between 1979 and 2007, for example. Immigrants in general and illegal aliens in particular tend to fall into the lower end of the job scale, because of their low education and skills levels. With figures like those above, it would seem impossible to justify either amnesty or a generous guest worker program. To do both would be unconscionable, at least from a biblically informed perspective. The most vulnerable of our national community would see 7-8 million jobs currently held by illegal aliens permanently tied up and those jobs foreclosed to jobless Americans. And "comprehensive immigration reform" would vastly increase the number of working-age immigrants legally brought into the country year after year into the future.

Another set of consequences of "comprehensive immigration reform" must also be carefully and fully considered. Those include the impact of legalizing 11 million illegal aliens on America's dire fiscal crisis.

Beneficiaries of amnesty would qualify for many public programs from which they currently are disqualified on account of their unlawful presence. Those programs include welfare, health care, the earned income tax credit, and entitlement programs. Because illegal aliens are predominately less educated and unskilled, they would disproportionately participate in these programs and collect far more in benefits than they would ever contribute in taxes.

This means native-born American taxpayers would effectively be required to subsidize foreign-born public program participation, on an even larger scale. It also means enriching former illegal aliens at the expense of lawful immigrants who played by the rules.

Consider the fiscal impact of "comprehensive immigration reform" on just one entitlement program, Medicaid. While illegal aliens are excluded from Medicaid, many would in all likelihood become eligible when they gained legal immigration status under amnesty. Under the recently enacted health reform, Medicaid is expanded substantially. In 2014, those with incomes up to 133 percent of the official poverty level will qualify for Medicaid. Analysis I have just completed indicates that 3.1 million current illegal aliens would have incomes that qualify them for Medicaid. They would add an extra $8.1 billion annually to the cost of the Medicaid program. In the budget window the Congressional Budget Office used for estimating health reform's costs, amnesty would cost taxpayers another $48.6 billion during the years 2014-2019.

The entire fiscal impact of amnesty and massively expanded immigration must be factored into the consideration of any immigration legislation. Rather than add to the nation's unsustainable fiscal obligations through immigration, it would be more fiscally responsible to reduce immigration and forego legalization.

In short, what "comprehensive immigration reform" would do unto "the least of these" fellow Americans hardly ranks as ethical treatment.

In closing, it would be unwise to misapply biblical principles in any public policy area. This is true with respect to immigration.

Immigration is one of those issues in which Scripture does not detail a normative public policy. This issue differs from clear-cut biblical precepts such as prohibiting murder, stealing, or perjury.

Thus, we have to consider which biblical principles do appropriately apply, carefully assess the situation at hand, consider this nation's experience and unique characteristics, judiciously estimate the impact of various policy options, and then exercise prudential judgment.

For biblical principles to inform our immigration policy, we must tread carefully. There is no proof text that justifies or mandates broad legalization, visas for certain countries or groups or skill levels, country quotas, or anything like that. Migration, where it comes up in Scripture, is incidental. The most precise teachings relate to fair treatment of resident aliens. Those who assert a biblical imperative for enacting "comprehensive immigration reform" or a specific bill are skating on thin ice.

Thinking prudentially, we know that in 1986, we tried immigration reform that looked largely the same as today's proposals: amnesty with border enforcement and employer sanctions. Some 3 million illegal aliens were legalized, including a number suspected of doing so fraudulently. Within a decade, the illegal population had mushroomed to three times the 1986 amnesty level. The supposed enforcement measures failed to secure the border or shut down the jobs magnet, because of fundamental flaws that guaranteed failure. The most vulnerable Americans have suffered the consequences most severely. Then as now, what passed for "enforcement" mainly amounted to inputs — hire this many more border officers, etc. — and completely ignored requiring results — curb illegal entry to near zero, reduce visa overstays to near zero, achieve near zero attempted re-entries by those previously removed or excluded, reduce to near zero the number of illegal aliens holding American jobs, etc.

Pursuing essentially the same failed "solution" hardly measures up to prudence. Today's proposals punish our fellow Americans through forced "compassion" they cannot afford. Perhaps the most ethical thing Congress could do is to suspend most immigration, at least until unemployment rates return to pre-recession levels.

****

I believe we need to have compassion on those that are less fortunate than we are, however we also need to look in our own back yard and correct the neglect that so many are suffering. We are a most generous nation when it comes to foreign countries suffering from some disaster. We even have ex-presidents join in the efforts to raise money and goods to alleviate the suffering. Wouldn't it be nice to have them offer the same service to help our own?

I really feel for those children that are displayed on TV, showing the filth and terrible lifestyle they live in. We have the same abominable situations right here in the USA - the richest country on earth. Why can't we turn our attention to our own problems for just a little while and solve our own maladies?

Several years ago I agonized over who I should offer our small monthly contribution to and then it dawned on me that contributing to one of our own institutions would also help the entire world since we always offer our knowledge to others.

We have a large problem in this country with immigration. Even if these illegals were given citizenship, it would not change their attitudes toward this country. They are still fighting the Mexican/American war and will continue to do so regardless of their status.

We have engrained in them over many years that they are entitled to a great many benefits and if they feel those benefits are being threatened, they display their true feelings. The following is just an example:

**

Montebello High School in California

You will not see this heart-stopping photo on the front page of the NY Times, nor on the lead story of the major news networks. The protestors at Montebello High School took the American flag off the school's flag pole and hung it upside down while putting up the Mexican flag over it. (*See pictures below*)

I predict this stunt will be the nail in the coffin of any guest-worker/ amnesty plan on the table in Washington ... The image of the American flag subsumed to another and turned upside down on American soil is already spreading on Internet forums and via e-mail.

Pass this along to every American citizen in your address books and to every representative in the state and federal government.. If you choose to remain uninvolved, do not be amazed when you no longer have a nation to call your own nor anything you have worked for left since it will be 'redistributed' to the activists while you are so peacefully staying out of the 'fray'. Check history, it is full of nations/empires that disappeared when its citizens no longer held their core beliefs and values. One person CAN make a difference....

One plus one plus one plus one plus one plus one........ ..

The battle for our secure borders and immigration laws that actually mean some-thing, however, hasn't even begun.

 HOPE this ticks YOU off....IF IT DOESN'T, IT SHOULD!

****

**

IT'S NO WONDER THE WORLD'S OUTLAWS AND PARASITES LAUGH AT US.

Parkland   Memorial Hospital in Dallas, Texas is a fairly famous institution and for a variety of reasons:

1. John F.. Kennedy died there in 1963
2. Lee Harvey Oswald died there shortly after
3. Jack Ruby-who killed Lee Harvey Os-wald, died there a few years later..by co-incidence

On the flip side, Parkland is also home to the second busiest maternity ward in the country with almost 16,000 new babies ar-riving each year.   (That's almost 44 per day---every day)

A recent patient survey indicated that 70 percent of the women who gave birth at Parkland in the first three months of 2006 were illegal immigrants. That's 11,200 anchor babies born every year just in Dallas .

According to the article, the hospital spent $70.7 million delivering 15,938 babies in 2004 but managed to end up with almost $8 million dollars in surplus funding. Medicaid kicked in $34.5 million, Dallas County taxpayers kicked in $31.3 million and the feds tossed in another $9.5 million..

The average patient in Parkland is maternity wards is 25 years old, married and giving birth to her second child. She is also an illegal immigrant. By law, pregnant women cannot be denied medical care based on their immigration status or ability to pay.

OK, fine. That doesn't mean they should receive better care than everyday, middle-class American citizens. But at Parkland Hospital, they do." Parkland Memorial Hospital has nine prenatal clinics. NINE.

The Dallas Morning News article followed a Hispanic woman who was a patient at one of the clinics and pregnant with her third child---her previous two were also born at Parkland. Her first two deliveries were free and the Mexican native was grateful because it would have cost $200 to have them in Mexico. This time, the hospital wants her to pay $10 per visit and $100 for the delivery but she was unsure if she could come up with the money. Not that it matters, the hospital won't turn her away. (I wonder why they even bother asking at this point..)

"How long has this been going on? What are the long-term effects?

Well, another subject of the article was born at Parkland in 1986 shortly after her mother entered the US illegally - now she is having her own child there as well. (That's right, she's technically a US citizen.)

These women receive free prenatal care including medication, nutrition, birthing classes and child care classes. They also get freebies such as car seats, bottles, diapers and formula.

Most of these things are available to American citizens as well but only for low-income applicants and even then, the red tape involved is almost insurmountable.

Because these women are illegal immigrants, they do not have to provide any sort of legitimate identification - no proof of income. An American citizen would have to provide a social security number which would reveal their annual income - an illegal immigrant need only claim to be poor and the hospital must take them at their word.

Parkland Hospital offers indigent care to Dallas County residents who earn less than $40,000 per year. (They also have to prove that they did not refuse health coverage at their current job. Yeah, the 'free' care is not so easy for Americans.)

There are about 140 patients who received roughly $4 million dollars for un-reimbursed medical care. As it turns out, they did not qualify for free treatment because they resided outside of Dallas County so the hospital is going to sue them! Illegals get it all free! But U. S citizens who live outside of Dallas County get sued! How stupid is this?

As if that isn't annoying enough, the illegal immigrant patients are actually complaining about hospital staff not speaking Spanish. In this AP story, the author speaks with a woman who is upset that she had to translate comments from the hospital staff into Spanish for her husband. The doctor was trying to explain the situation to the family and the mother was forced to translate for her husband who only spoke Spanish. This was apparently a great injustice to her.

In an attempt to create a Spanish-speaking staff, Parkland Hospital is now providing incentives in the form of extra pay for applicants who speak Spanish. Additionally, medical students at the University of Texas Southwestern for which Parkland Hospital is the training facility will

now have a Spanish language requirement added to their already jammed-
packed curriculum. No other school in the
country boasts such a ridiculous multi-
semester (multicultural) requirement.

(Sorry for the length, but this needs wide
circulation particularly to our "employees"
in Congress...)

Remember that this is about only ONE
hospital in Dallas, Texas . There are many
more hospitals across our country that
must also deal with this.

If you want to verify accuracy:

http://www.snopes.com/politics/immigrati
on/parkland.asp

                  ****

                  **

A wise man once said all that has to happen is for wise men to do NOTHING!!!

The message is clear.....Do nothing and you will have nothing!! It seems apparent that the present administration has set out to destroy America as we know it!!

FORMER GOVERNOR GIVES US A FORE-WARNING !

IN GOD WE TRUST

Wherever you stand, please take the time to read this; it ought to scare the pants off you!

We know Dick Lamm as the former Governor of Colorado.

In that context, his thoughts are particularly poignant. Last week there was an immigration overpopulation conference in Washington, DC, filled to capacity by many of America's finest minds and leaders. A brilliant college professor by the name of Victor Hansen Davis talked about his latest book, 'Mexifornia,' explaining how immigration - both legal and illegal was destroying the entire state of California. He said it would march across the country until it destroyed all vestiges of The American Dream.

Moments later, former Colorado Governor Richard D. Lamm stood up and gave a stunning speech on how to destroy America. The audience sat spellbound as he described eight methods for the destruction of the United States. He said, 'If you believe that America is too smug, too self-satisfied, too rich, then let's destroy America. It is not that hard to do. No nation in history has survived the ravages of time.

Arnold Toynbee observed that all great civilizations rise and fall and that 'An autopsy of history would show that all great nations commit suicide."

'Here is how they do it,' Lamm said: 'First, to destroy America, turn America into a bilingual or multi-lingual and bicultural country.' History shows that no nation can survive the tension, conflict, and antagonism of two or more competing languages and cultures. It is a blessing for an individual to be bilingual; however, it is a curse for a society to be bilingual.

The historical scholar, Seymour Lipset, put it this way: 'The histories of bilingual and bicultural societies that do not assimilate are histories of turmoil, tension, and tragedy.' Canada, Belgium, Malaysia, and Lebanon all face crises of national existence in which minorities press for autonomy, if not independence. Pakistan and Cyprus have divided. Nigeria suppressed an ethnic rebellion. France faces difficulties with Basques, Bretons, and Corsicans.'

Lamm went on: Second, to destroy America , 'Invent 'multiculturalism' and encourage immigrants to maintain their culture. Make it an article of belief that all cultures are equal That there are no cultural differences. Make it an article of faith that the Black and Hispanic dropout rates are due solely to prejudice and discrimination by the majority. Every other explanation is out of bounds.

Third, 'We could make the United States an 'Hispanic Quebec' without much effort. The key is to celebrate diversity rather than unity. As Benjamin Schwarz said in the Atlantic Monthly recently: 'The apparent success of our own multiethnic and multicultural experiment might have been achieved not by tolerance but by hegemony. Without the dominance that once dictated ethnocentricity and what it meant to be an American, we are left with only tolerance and pluralism to hold us together.'

Lamm said, 'I would encourage all immigrants to keep their own language and culture I would replace the melting pot metaphor with the salad bowl metaphor. It is important to ensure that we have various cultural subgroups living in America enforcing their differences rather than as Americans, emphasizing their similarities.'

'Fourth, I would make our fastest growing demographic group the least educated. I would add a second underclass, unassimilated, under-educated, and antagonistic to our population. I would have this second underclass have a 50% dropout rate from high school.'

'My fifth point for destroying America would be to get big foundations and business to give these efforts lots of money. I would invest in ethnic identity, and I would establish the cult of 'Victimology.' I would get all minorities to think that their lack of success was the fault of the majority. I would start a grievance industry blaming all minority failure on the majority population.'

'My sixth plan for America's downfall would include dual citizenship, and promote divided loyalties. I would celebrate diversity over unity. I would stress differences rather than similarities. Diverse people worldwide are mostly engaged in hating each other - that is, when they are not killing each other. A diverse, peaceful, or stable society is against most historical precedent. People undervalue the unity it takes to keep a nation together. Look at the ancient Greeks. The Greeks believed that they belonged to the same race; they possessed a common Language and literature; and they worshipped the same gods. All Greece took part in the Olympic games. A common enemy, Persia, threatened their liberty. Yet all these bonds were not strong enough to overcome two factors: local patriotism and geographical conditions that nurtured political divisions. Greece fell. 'E. Pluribus Unum'

From many, one. In that historical reality, if we put the emphasis on the 'pluribus' instead of the 'Unum,' we will balkanize America as surely as Kosovo.'

'Next to last, I would place all subjects off limits; make it taboo to talk about anything against the cult of 'diversity.' I would find a word similar to 'heretic' in the 16th century - that stopped discussion and paralyzed thinking. Words like 'racist' or 'xenophobe' halt discussion and debate.

Having made America a bilingual/bicultural country, having established multi-culturism, having the large foundations fund the doctrine of 'Victimology,' I would next make it impossible to enforce our immigration laws. I would develop a mantra: That because immigration has been good for America , it must always be good. I would make every individual immigrant symmetric and ignore the cumulative impact of millions of them.'

In the last minute of his speech, Governor Lamm wiped his brow.

Profound silence followed. Finally he said,. 'Lastly, I would censor Victor Hanson

Davis's book 'Mexifornia.' His book is dangerous. It exposes the plan to destroy America . If you feel America deserves to be destroyed, don't read that book.'

There was no applause. A chilling fear quietly rose like an ominous cloud above every attendee at the conference. Every American in that room knew that everything Lamm enumerated was proceeding methodically, quietly, darkly, yet pervasively across the United States today.

Discussion is being suppressed. Over 100 languages are ripping the foundation of our educational system and national cohesiveness. Even barbaric cultures that practice female genital mutilation are growing as we celebrate 'diversity.' American jobs are vanishing into the Third World as corporations create a Third World in America - take note of California and other states - to date, ten million illegal aliens and growing fast. It is reminiscent of George Orwell's book '1984.' In that story, three slogans are engraved in the Ministry of Truth building: 'War is peace,' 'Freedom is slavery,' and 'Ignorance is strength.'

Governor Lamm walked back to his seat. It dawned on everyone at the conference that our nation and the future of this great democracy is deeply in trouble and worsening fast. If we don't get this immigration monster stopped within three years, it will rage like a California wildfire and destroy everything in its path especially The American Dream.

DO NOTHING AND YOU WILL HAVE NOTHING!

****

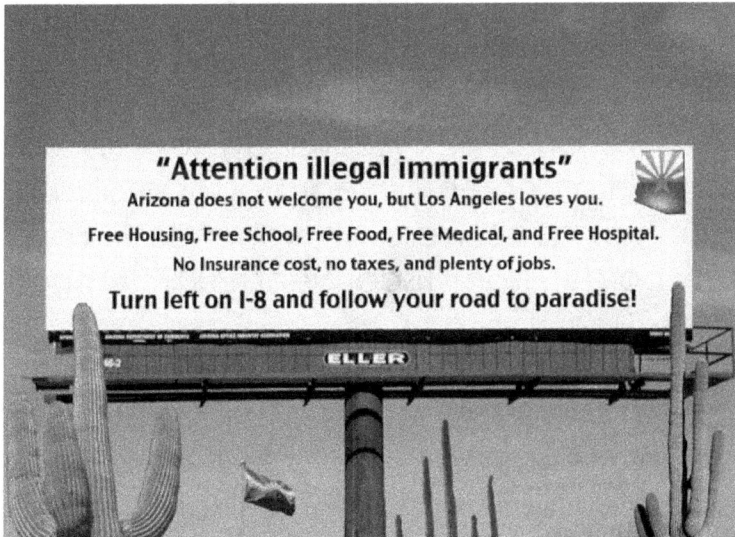

I don't seem to run out of material on this subject. I will insert several more emails on immigration.

**

US-Mexico Border Easy Entry for Terrorists

Friday, 25 Jun 2010 08:42 AM

By: Deroy Murdock

While Americans march against Arizona's new restrictions on unlawful immigration, hundreds of illegal aliens from countries awash in Muslim terrorists tiptoe across the U.S.-Mexican frontier.

New York, N.Y. — According to the federal Enforcement Integrated Database, 125 individuals were apprehended along the border from fiscal year 2009 through April 20, 2010.

These deportable aliens included two Syrians, seven Sudanese, and 17 Iranians, all nationals from the three Islamic countries that the U.S. government officially classifies as state sponsors of terrorism.

Federal authorities also track "special interest countries" from which terrorism could be directed against America. Over the aforementioned period, 99 of those nations' citizens also were nabbed on the border.

They were two Afghans, five Algerians, 13 Iraqis, 10 Lebanese, 22 Nigerians, 28 Pakistanis, two Saudis, 14 Somalis, and three Yemenis. During FY 2007 and FY 2008, federal officials caught 319 people from these same countries traversing America's southwest border.

Some such characters were confined in Arizona, which recently adopted a controversial law that lets cops ask the citizenship status of those they suspect of other possible violations.

WSB-TV recently publicized an April 15, 2010, "population breakdown" of immigrants detained at a facility in Florence, Ariz. Of the 395 males behind bars, 198 were Mexican, 18 hailed from Afghanistan, Iraq, Iran, Lebanon, Nigeria, Pakistan, Somalia, Sudan and Yemen.

Perhaps these gentlemen simply want to pursue the American dream.

Worrisome signs suggest, however, that some may have arrived via blistering, cactus-adorned deserts so they could blow Americans to smithereens.

Texas Border Patrol agents discovered, along with Iranian currency and Islamic prayer rugs, an Arabic clothing patch that reads "martyr" and "way to immortality."

Another shows a jet flying into a skyscraper.

"Members of Hezbollah, the Lebanon-based terrorist organization, have already entered the United States across our southwest border," declares "A Line in the Sand," a 2006 report by the House Homeland Security Investigations Subcommittee, then-chaired by Rep. Michael McCaul, R-Texas.

Even more disturbing are the uninvited terrorists and terror suspects that were arrested after entering America through our permeable underbelly:

Mahmoud Youssef Kourani pleaded guilty in March 2005 to providing material support to terrorists. First, Kourani secured a visa by bribing a Mexican diplomat in Beirut. He and another Middle Easterner then hired a Mexican guide to escort them into America. Finally, Kourani settled in Dearborn, Michigan's Lebanese-immigrant community, and raised cash for Hezbollah.

Miguel Alfonso Salinas was caught in New Mexico near the international border in 2006. As The Washington Examiner reported, one week of FBI interrogation exposed Salinas as an Egyptian named Ayman Sulmane Kamal. Evidently, he remains in federal custody.

Then-National Intelligence Director Mike McConnell said that in FY 2006 and FY 2007, at least 30 potentially dangerous Iraqis were found trying to penetrate America via Mexico. As McConnell told the El Paso Times: "There are numerous situations where people are alive today because we caught them." — The Department of Homeland Security issued an April 14 intelligence alert regarding a possible border-crossing attempt by a Somali named Mohamed Ali. He is a suspected member of Al-Shabaab, a Somali-based al-Qaida ally tied to the deadly attack on American GIs in 1993's notorious "Blackhawk Down" incident in Mogadishu.

Captured in Brownsville, Texas, Ahmed Muhammed Dhakane pleaded not guilty on May 14 to federal charges that he "ran a large-scale smuggling enterprise" designed to sneak East Africans through Mexico into Texas, including "several AIAI-affiliated Somalis into the United States." Al-Ittihad Al-Islami is yet another Muslim-extremist organization.

Daniel Joseph Maldonado also has Somali ties. He was picked up in Somalia in 2007 during terrorist training. He was returned to Houston for prosecution. As Rice University's Joan Neuhas Schaan told KHOU-TV: "They had plans for him to come back to the United States and recruit female suicide bombers."

All this involves only the bad guys who the authorities nailed. Those who have stayed undetected after crossing the border to murder Americans remain, by definition, invisible.

****

**

The following was a letter to the editor of the LA Times. I must say he is a little ticked off, as if you can't tell.

Hector,

I can't believe that a major metropolitan paper like the LA Times would publish drivel like your distortion-laden column I had the misfortune to read today. The citizens of Arizona passed a law that makes it necessary to prove you are in their state LEGALLY. They are tired of paying TWO BILLION taxpayer dollars a year in medical and educational benefits to people in their state ILLEGALLY. They are tired of the Mexican drug traffickers, kidnappings (389 last year), traffic accidents, and crime caused by ILLEGAL immigrants in their state. They are tired of citizens of a foreign country overcrowding and bankrupting their emergency rooms and schools. They have the ABSOLUTE RIGHT to defend their state when the federal government fails to do so just like I have the right to put three hollow-points in the chest of the guy who's trying to kick in my front door when the cops don't show up.

It has been the law in this country since 1940 that foreign nationals be able to produce proof that they are here LEGALLY by way of visa, green card, etc. This "Produce your papers" and the allusions to Nazi Germany is a bunch of dishonest claptrap. If you took time to read the Arizona law (assuming you can read English) you would see that police officers may only inquire as to an individual's immigration status in the course of a "legal contact". The problem with you and Mexicans like you is the fact that you have this sense of entitlement that you can enter OUR COUNTRY as you please. You come from a culture and a country with no respect for the law or the rule of law. The United States is a sovereign nation with the ABSOLUTE RIGHT to decide who does and does not enter our country.

What amuses me the most is the fact that if our illegal immigration problem was due to the influx of SWEDES, you wouldn't have written ONE WORD in the defense of their rights. It is only because they are Hispanics like you that you leap to their defense. I find it ironic that you are truer to your Hispanic roots than you are to your American citizenship, especially since the Hispanic culture is a broke-dick, busted-ass, ignorant-ass, uneducated, going-nowhere culture and has been for the last 500 years, and in all likelihood, will be for the NEXT 500 years.

When I moved to California in 1969, Los Angeles was a clean prosperous city. Now it's broke under the weight of massive entitlements. Now we need concertina wire to protect our freeway signs from Hispano-moron graffiti "artists'. What an enlightened culture you come from that believes that vandalizing another's property is an art form. Over 400 California families have lost loved ones to ILLEGAL immigrant murderers. 40% of the criminals incarcerated in our prisons at CALIFORNIA TAXPAYER EXPENSE, are ILLEGAL immigrants. Thank you so much for our overcrowded ERs, schools and freeways. Thanks also for the gangs and the drive-by shootings. In all fairness though, I like the tacos.

If I want to enter Mexico , France , England , Germany or ANY country on this earth, I need to produce a passport to do so. It's THEIR COUNTRY and I need to ask permission to do so. HOW DARE you and your brethren think that they have some God-given right to flout our laws and come into our country of their own accord. You and people like you are the textbook example of why the fewer Mexicans we have in our country, the better our country will be. We manage to produce a steady supply of home-grown idiots on our own, thank very much (Exhibit A - Obama)

Good luck with your boycotts and your protests. Just remember; amigo, 70% of the people in Arizona and 65% of Americans LOVE this law. Every time you put together thousands of protesters, you piss off MILLIONS of people like me.

Hasta la vista, baby.

Tom Edwards

****

I just received several pictures that will drive home the mentality of our "south of the border" friends. This has really got to take the cake. Just imagine your grandmother doing this. These pictures almost make you sick. Now for just a moment, think about those that buy this stuff and smoke it - or whatever. I wonder how much she was paid for this "job?" I also pity to poor border guards that have to "inspect" people like this to do their job. And we complain about taking our shoes off at the airport. :

**

How to bring in drugs from Mexico.

Now you can't help but feel sorry for this poooooooorrr soul!!!!

And here you have an industrious Mexican national, just simply on her way to visiting her friends and relatives across the international border in Arizona, all the while passing through the port of entry at Nogales, Arizona probably daily.

After all, she's only 94 years old, so what harm could this Mexican do. Well I'll be dipped. What's all that padded stuff affixed to her body, underneath her dress. Well, after the dress was removed, loooookeeee here at what we have.

Why it's only 10.45 pounds of marijuana strapped to her body. Can we blame her, after all, she's probably just supplementing her social security check she gets monthly at her P.O. box on the American side. And one can't help but wonder how many of these such trips has she already made across the border, toting 10 3/4 pounds of marijuana daily. Hang it up lady, as it's time for you to retire permanently in Mexico.

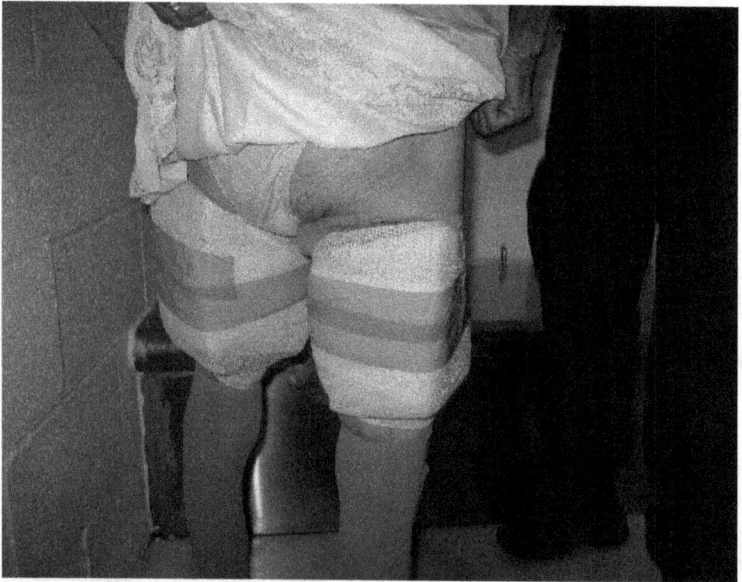

One Candle at a Time

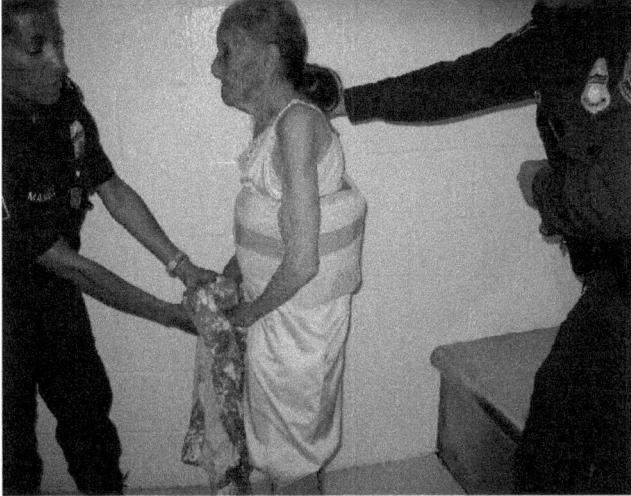

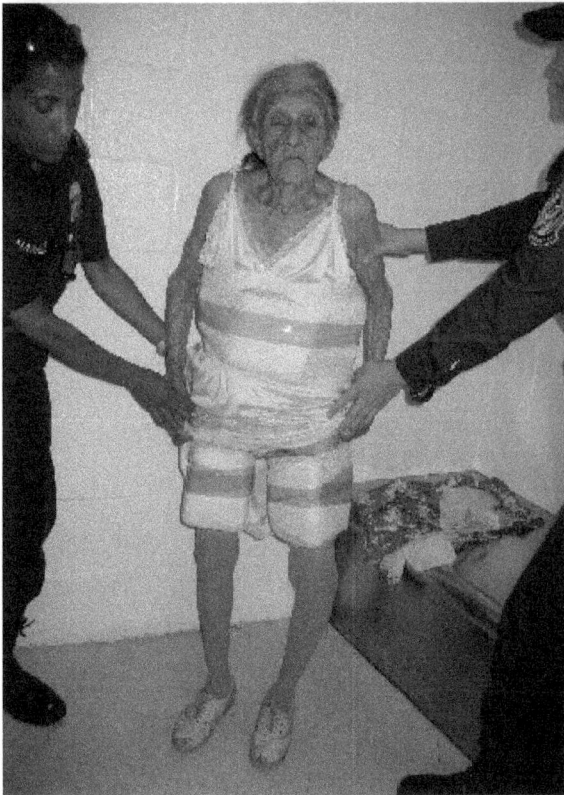

Excuse me while I throw up!

And God Created Pennsylvania ....

God was missing for six days. Eventually, Michael, the archangel, found him, resting on the seventh day.

He inquired, "Where have you been?" God smiled deeply and proudly pointed downwards through the clouds, "Look, Michael. Look what I've made."

Archangel Michael looked puzzled, and said, "What is it?" "It's a planet," replied God, and I've put life on it. I'm going to call it Earth and it's going to be a place to test Balance."

"Balance?" inquired Michael, "I'm still confused." God explained, pointing to different parts of Earth.

"For example, northern Europe will be a place of great opportunity and wealth, while southern Europe is going to be poor. Over here I've placed a continent of white people, and over there is a continent of black people. Balance in all things."

God continued pointing to different countries. "This one will be extremely hot, while this one will be very cold and covered in ice."

The Archangel , impressed by God's work, then pointed to a land area and said, "What's that one?" "That's Pennsylvania , the most glorious place on earth. There are beautiful mountains, rivers and streams, lakes, forests, hills, and plains.

The people from Pennsylvania are going to be handsome, modest, intelligent, and humorous, and they are going to travel the world. They will be extremely sociable, hardworking, high achieving, carriers of peace, and producers of good things."

Michael gasped in wonder and admiration, but then asked, "But what about balance, God? You said there would be balance." God smiled, "Not very far from Pennsylvania is Washington, DC. Wait till you see the idiots I put there."

Arizona

Molly Brown
by Florence Markoff

The story of how she got rich and survived the sinking of the Titanic.

Margaret Tobin Brown in 1900.

The year was 1912. The United States was growing; two more stars were added to the national flag as New Mexico and Arizona joined the union. The Girl Scouts of America was founded in Savannah, Georgia, by Juliette Low. With Camille, starring the world-famous actress, the divine Sarah Bernhardt, the motion picture industry began to flourish; and a spunky Irish woman sang the popular song of the day, "When Irish Eyes are Smiling." Her name was Molly Brown.

Now Molly Brown loved to tell a good story, and when she moved to Newport and rubbed elbows with the rich folk there she entertained them with tales of her adventures and how she struck it rich. She told the stories over and over, and the people who heard them said she was a real honest-to-goodness heroine.

Molly told how she went to Leadville, Colorado, at the height of the Gold Rush boom. There she married Johnny Brown—Leadville Johnny they called him—and lived with him in his little cabin in the hills. When he struck gold and was offered three hundred thousand dollars for his claim, he accepted on one condition: "Pay me in thousand dollar bills. I want to take it home and throw it in the lap of my beautiful wife." He gave Molly the money—all of it—and left for the town saloon to celebrate his good fortune. When he returned, he fetched some kindling wood to start a fire. Molly saw what he was doing and screamed, but it was too late. She had hidden the money in the stove and her $300,000 went up the flue.

But Leadville Johnny didn't worry. There was lots more where that came from. His mine became one of the greatest producers of gold in Colorado history, and the Browns began to live it up. Molly bedecked herself in furs and jewels and moved on to the rich social life of Newport, where she amused the people of wealth with her bad jokes, loud expensive parties, and stories of her early days. They were just the thing to liven up a dull dinner party.

It didn't take long for Molly to get fancy—she traveled with the international set—and on a special day in April 1912 she was on the palatial $7,500,000 White Star liner called the Titanic. It was on its maiden voyage from Southampton, England, to New York with 2,223 passengers. When the Titanic struck an iceberg on that bitter cold night and the ship was sinking, Molly boarded lifeboat number 6 in her sable coat, grabbed an oar, and got the frightened passengers to sing... "When Irish Eyes Are Smiling."

Thanks to Molly, no one died in boat number 6. "I'm unsinkable," she declared to waiting reporters in New York. And ever after, when stories of bravery on the Titanic are told, they always talk about the woman from Newport with the indomitable spirit who called herself... the unsinkable Molly Brown.

Not many people have heard all the details of this story - except that she was on the Titanic when it sank. Molly was a tough gal and so are the people of Arizona even if the Federal Government is suing them over their newly adopted immigration law. See some more emails regarding this situation:

**

National Support for Arizona Remains High

On Thursday, we learned that Secretary of State Hillary Clinton told a television station in Ecuador that the Obama Administration will indeed sue the state of Arizona over its new immigration enforcement law. Americans continue to disagree with the Administration's view, however. A brand new Washington Post/ABC News poll reveals that nearly <u>60% of Americans support Arizona's new law</u>.

According to the poll, the majority of Americans do believe that immigration enforcement should be handled by the federal government and not the states, but a majority of Americans recognize the federal government's unwillingness to enforce immigration laws and disapprove of Pres. Obama's handling of the immigration issue. And 83% of Americans believe that the National Guard should be patrolling the border. Last month, Pres. Obama <u>sent 1,200 troops to the border</u> in a non-patrolling role.

Thanks,
Chris Chmielenski   ****
Website Content Manager

**

Pictures from the illegal's protest march in Phoenix Memorial Day is a day to honor those who give their lives for our nation.

This is what we had in Phoenix courtesy of the Mexicans and the SEIU

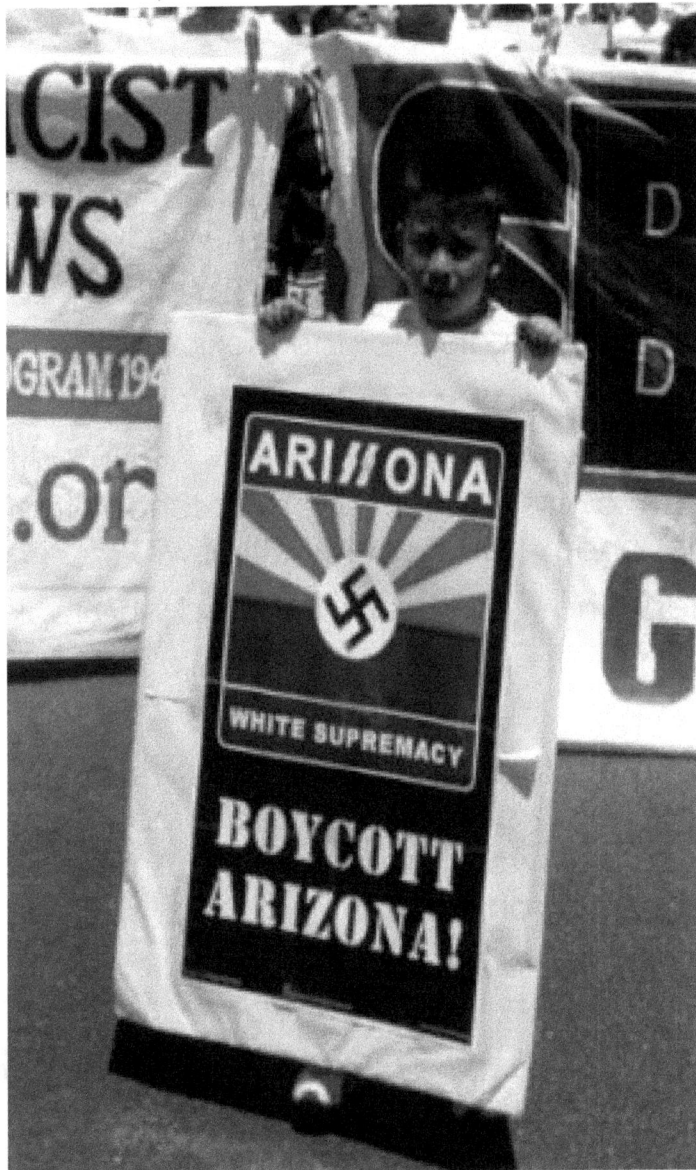

****

**

My great grandfather watched as his friends died in the Civil War, my father watched as his friends died in WW II, and I watched as my friends died in Vietnam ..

None of them died for the Mexican Flag.

Everyone died for the U.S. flag.

Just this week, here in Texas , a student raised a Mexican flag on a school flag pole; another student took it down.

Guess who was expelled..the kid who took it down.

Kids in high school in California were sent home this week on Cinco de Mayo because they wore T-shirts with the American flag printed on them.

Enough is enough.

Every American needs to stand up for America. We've bent over to appease the America-haters long enough. I'm taking a stand.

I'm standing up because the hundreds of thousands who died fighting in wars for this country, and for the U.S. flag can't stand up.

And shame on anyone who tries to make this a racist message.

Sandy Tucker

Bulverde, Texas

****

**

ARIZONA / CALIFORNIA LAW THE SAME-IMPORTANT

My name is Harold R. Beasley, Sr. I am a retired Border Patrol Agent. I live in Sierra Vista, AZ. Telephone number 520-459-8587. I was the Deputy Chief Patrol Agent in San Diego for 5 years (1996 to 2001). I then transferred as an Assistant Chief Patrol Agent to Tucson, Arizona and then retired in 2002.

I did a little research and found that California has the same law (Penal Code 834b) on their books and are complaining about Arizona just passing our New Immigration Law. Wow, is this the pot calling the kettle black?

Please note the last section 834(b)(c). Looks like Los Angeles and San Francisco Mayors have violated California Law and should be investigated by the Attorney General of California.

Below is the message that I sent to the Mayors of Los Angeles and San Francisco:

You are fighting the new Arizona Immigration Law. Well take a good look at your laws over in California. You are telling Arizona that we are racists and will be racial profiling. Read California Penal Code 834b. You are violating your own State Laws by not enforcing Penal Code 834b. You have had the same law for many years and NO ONE has been protesting your law. WHY IS THAT?

834b. (a) Every law enforcement agency in California shall fully cooperate with the United States Immigration and Naturalization Service regarding any person who is arrested if he or she is suspected of being present in the United States in violation of federal immigration laws.

(b) With respect to any such person who is arrested, and suspected of being present in the United States in violation of federal immigration laws, every law enforcement agency shall do the following:

(1) Attempt to verify the legal status of such person as a citizen of the United States, an alien lawfully admitted as a permanent resident, an alien lawfully admitted for a temporary period of time or as an alien who is present in the United States in violation of immigration laws. The verification process may include, but shall not be limited to, questioning the person regarding his or her date and place of birth, and entry into the United States, and demanding documentation to indicate his or her legal status.

(2) Notify the person of his or her apparent status as an alien who is present in the United States in violation of federal immigration laws and inform him or her that, apart from any criminal justice proceedings, he or she must either obtain legal status or leave the United States.

(3) Notify the Attorney General of California and the United States Immigration and Naturalization Service of the apparent illegal status and provide any additional information that may be requested by any other public entity.

(4) Any legislative, administrative, or other action by a city, county, or other legally authorized local governmental entity with jurisdictional boundaries, or by a law enforcement agency, to prevent or limit the cooperation required by subdivision (a) is expressly prohibited.

****

I'm sure that many of you watched the Phoenix Suns play basketball recently and noticed something slightly different about their uniforms. The players took the side of the protesters in the wearing of this change in uniform. The following is a note from the Governor of Arizona:

**

Subject: FW: from the governor of AZ

Referring to the Phoenix Suns basketball team for those of you in Rio Linda... J

How would the Sun's owners like it if ...

"What if the owners of the Suns discovered that hordes of people were sneaking into games without paying? What if they had a good idea who the gate-crashers are, but the ushers and security personnel were not allowed to ask these folks to produce their ticket stubs, thus non-paying attendees couldn't be ejected. Furthermore, what if Suns' ownership was expected to provide those who sneaked in with complimentary eats and drink? And what if, on those days when a gate-crasher became ill or injured, the Suns had to provide free medical care and shelter?" - This was posted by Arizona Gov. Jan Brewer on FaceBook, I love the analogy to illegal aliens. I wish this lady would run for president!

****

**

This vehicle was stopped in Arizona, from Texas - in route to California.

One Candle at a Time

How many new ways can they come up with to deliver the "goods"? Then there are those that have proclaimed our borders are safe.

The United State of America

Sanctuary

ARIZONA

Artizans.com CultureandMediaInstitute.org

**

Back during The Great Depression, President Herbert Hoover ordered the deportation of ALL illegal aliens in order to make jobs available to American citizens that desperately needed work..

Harry Truman deported over two million Illegal's after WWII to create jobs for returning veterans.

And then again in 1954, President Dwight Eisenhower deported 13 million Mexican Nationals! The program was called 'Operation Wetback'. It was done so WWII and Korean Veterans would have a better chance at jobs. It took 2 Years, but they deported them!

Confirm: http://en.wikipedia.org/wiki/Operation_Wetback

Now...if they could deport the illegal's back then - they could sure do it today?

If you have doubts about the veracity of this information, enter Operation Wetback into your favorite search engine and confirm it for yourself.

Reminder: Don't forget to pay your taxes... 32 million Illegal Aliens are depending on you!

Deport my voters? NEVER!

****

Leave it to Maxine to put things in perspective:

**

I bought a bird feeder. I hung It on my back porch and filled It with seed. What a beauty of a bird feeder it was, as I filled it lovingly with seed. Within a week we had hundreds of birds taking advantage of the continuous flow of free and easily accessible food.

But then the birds started building nests in the boards of the patio, above the table, And next to the barbecue.

Then came the poop. It was everywhere: on the patio tile, The chairs, the table .. Everywhere!

Then some of the birds turned mean. They would dive bomb me and try to peck me even though I had fed them out of my own pocket.

And others birds were boisterous and loud. They sat on the feeder and squawked and screamed at all hours of the day and night and demanded that I fill it when it got low on food.

After a while, I couldn't even sit on my own back porch anymore.   So I took down the bird feeder and in three days The birds were gone. I cleaned up their mess and took down the many nests they had built all over the patio.

Soon, the back yard was like It used to be .... Quiet, serene.... And no one demanding their rights to a free meal.

Now let's see. Our government gives out free food, subsidized housing, free medical care and free education, and allows anyone born here to be an automatic citizen.

Then the illegal's came by the tens of thousands. Suddenly our taxes went up to pay for free services; small apartments are housing 5 families; you have to wait 6 hours to be seen by an emergency room doctor; Your child's second grade class is behind other schools because over half the class doesn't speak English.

Corn Flakes now come in a bilingual box; I have to 'press one ' to hear my bank talk to me in English, and people waving flags other than 'Old Glory' are squawking and screaming In the streets, demanding more rights and free liberties.

Just my opinion, but maybe it's time for the government to take down the bird feeder.

If you agree, pass it on; if not, Just continue cleaning up the poop.

****

May God grant us the stamina to withstand this onslaught of evil.

<u>Let's keep a candle burning for Arizona!</u>

Our Government

Why are all these things happening to us now? Is it because we've waited too long to do something about them? Is it because we haven't given our representatives the right directives or we've kept them there too long and now they feel entitled to act the way they do? Maybe it's because we've sent the wrong people to Washington to do our bidding!

Just last week, Senator Byrd from West Virginia died. Robert Carlyle Byrd (born Cornelius Calvin Sale, Jr.; November 20, 1917 – June 28, 2010) was a United States Senator from West Virginia. A member of the Democratic Party, Byrd served as a Senator from 1959 to 2010 and was the longest-serving senator and the longest-serving member in the history of the United States Congress.

Initially elected to the United States House of Representatives in 1952, Byrd served there for six years before being elected to the Senate in 1958. He rose to become one of the most powerful members of the Senate, serving as secretary of the Senate Democratic Caucus from 1967 to 1971 and – after defeating his longtime colleague, Edward Kennedy – as Senate Majority Whip from 1971 to 1977. Byrd led the Democratic caucus as Senate Majority Leader from 1977 to 1981 and 1987 to 1989, and as Senate Minority Leader from 1981 to 1987. From 1989 to 2010 he served as the President pro tempore of the United States Senate when the Democratic Party had a majority, and as President pro tempore emeritus during periods of Republican majority beginning in 2001. As President pro tempore, he was third in the line of presidential succession, behind the Vice President and the Speaker of the House of Representatives. He also served as the Chairman of the United States Senate Committee on Appropriations from 1989 to 1995, 2001 to 2003, and 2007 to 2009, giving him extraordinary influence over federal spending.

Byrd's seniority and leadership of the Appropriations Committee enabled him to steer a great deal of federal money toward projects in West Virginia. Critics derided his efforts as pork spending designed simply to appeal to his own constituents. Over his career, he held a wide variety of both liberal and conservative political views, starting his career as a conservative Southern Democrat. He filibustered against the 1964 Civil Rights Act and supported the Vietnam War, but later backed civil rights measures and criticized the Iraq War. Rating his voting record in 1964, the liberal lobbying group Americans for Democratic Action found that his views and the organization's were aligned only 16 percent of the time, less than even conservative Republicans of the era; by 2005, he had an ADA rating of 95 percent. Conversely, the American Conservative Union rated Byrd a conservative in its first ratings in 1972.

This is a prime example of a representative of the people holding office too long. I'm sure he accomplished many good things during his reign, but 51 years in the Senate is about 40 to many.

When the people's interest, and the country's, is put aside in favor of a political solution - things have to change. Not only do the Democrats have these problems, but also the Republicans. The more I hear about political solutions I just know that half of the citizens are getting screwed.

Take for example: The election of 2000. The Presidential spot had to be decided by the courts. Maybe it would be better if the "winner" had to pick the "loser" to be Vice President.

In the Congress, eliminate Democrats and Republicans in favor of Conservative and Liberal groups. That way we would really know which side of the dollar bill they stood. Times are tough and they have changed over the years. All Democrats are not liberal and all Republicans are not conservative.   When the battle heats up they all claim to belong to the group that seems to be winning (thats called politics). It's really called "lying" to your face.

**

This man, 73, Is wearing a protective flap over his ear while Joe Biden, Barack Obama and Nancy Pelosi addressed the Veterans of Foreign Wars,

I wish I could shake this man's hand.

I just want to know where he got it.....?

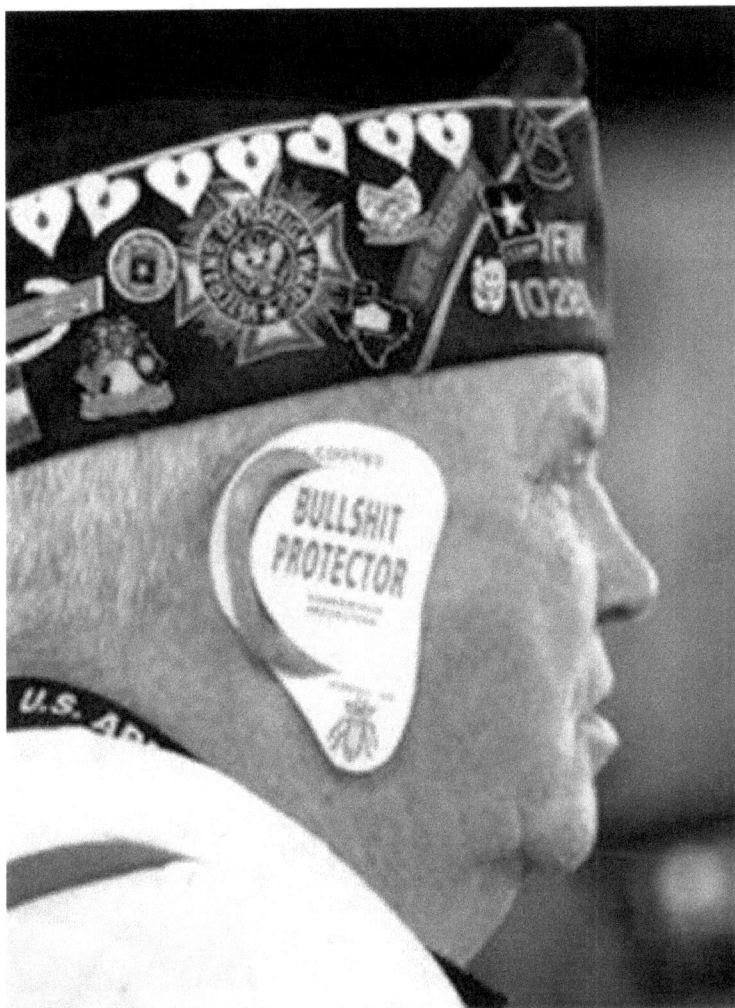

****

Where were these things when they started to campaign? It sure would have saved us a bunch or trouble.

Mr. BO is the smoothest lier this country has ever seen. I used to believe that President Carter was the worst - but, BO takes the cake.

I believe BO has lived on these pills for years.

I'm not the worst President anymore!!

Sorry Jimmy, you have lost your title.

**

The Fundamental Transformation of America

When Obama wrote a book and said he was mentored as a youth by Frank, (Frank Marshall Davis) an avowed Communist,
People said it didn't matter.

When it was discovered that his grandparents, were strong socialists, sent Obama's mother to a socialist school, introduced Frank Marshall Davis to young Obama,
People said it didn't matter.

When people found out that he was enrolled as a Muslim child in school and his father and step father were both Muslims,
People said it didn't matter.

When he wrote in another book he authored „I will stand with them (Muslims) should the political winds shift in an ugly direction.
People said it didn't matter.

When he admittedly, in his book,said he chose Marxist friends and professors in college,

People said it didn't matter.

When he traveled to Pakistan , after college on an unknown national passport,

People said it didn't matter.

When he sought the endorsement of the Marxist party in 1996 as he ran for the Illinois Senate,

People said it doesn't matter.

When he sat in a Chicago Church for twenty years and listened to a preacher spew hatred for America and preach black liberation theology,

People said it didn't matter.

When an independent Washington organization, that tracks senate voting records, gave him the distinctive title as the "most liberal senator",

People said it didn't matter.

When the Palestinians in Gaza , set up a
fund raising telethon to raise money for his
election campaign,

People said it didn't matter.

When his voting record supported gun
control,

People said it didn't matter.

When he refused to disclose who donated
money to his election campaign, as
other candidates had done,

People said it didn't matter.

When he received endorsements from
people like Louis Farrakhan and Mummar
Kadaffi and Hugo Chavez,

People said it didn't matter.

When it was pointed out that he was a total, newcomer and had absolutely no experience at anything except community
organizing,

People said it didn't matter.

When he chose friends and acquaintances such as Bill Ayers and Bernadine Dohrn who were revolutionary radicals,

People said it didn't matter.

When his voting record in the Illinois senate and in the U.S. Senate came into question,

People said it didn't matter.

When he refused to wear a flag, lapel pin and did so only after a public outcry,

People said it didn't matter.

When people started treating him as a Messiah and children in schools were taught to sing his praises,

People said it didn't matter.

When he stood with his hands over his groin area for the playing of the National Anthem and Pledge of Allegiance,

People said it didn't matter.

When he surrounded himself in the White house with advisors who were pro gun control, pro abortion, pro homosexual marriage and wanting to curtail freedom of speech to silence the opposition and when he aired his views on abortion, homosexuality and a host of other issues,

People said it didn't matter.

When he said he favors sex education in Kindergarten, including homosexual indoctrination,

People said it didn't matter.

When his background was either scrubbed or hidden and nothing could be found about him,

People said it didn't matter.

When the place of his birth was called into question, and he refused to produce a birth certificate,

People said it didn't matter.

Ron Berger 176

When he had an association in Chicago with Tony Rezco, a man of questionable character, who is now in prison and had helped Obama to a sweet deal on the purchase of his home,

People said it didn't matter.

When it became known that George Soros, a multi-billionaire Marxist, spent a ton of money to get him elected,

People said it didn't matter.

When he started appointing czars that were radicals, revolutionaries, and even avowed Marxist/Communist,

People said it didn't matter.

When he stood before the nation and told us that his intentions were to "fundamentally transform this nation" into something else,

People said it didn't matter.

When it became known that he had trained ACORN workers in Chicago and served as an attorney for ACORN,

People said it didn't matter.

When he appointed cabinet members and several advisors who were tax cheats and socialist,
People said it didn't matter.

When he appointed a science czar, John Holdren, who believes in forced abortions, mass sterilizations and seizing babies from teen mothers,
People said it didn't matter.

When he appointed Cass Sunstein as regulatory czar and he believes in "Explicit Consent", harvesting human organs without family consent, and to allow animals to be represented in court, while banning all hunting,
People said it didn't matter.

When he appointed Kevin Jennings, a homosexual, and organizer of a group called gay, lesbian, straight, Education network, as safe school czar and it became known that he had a history of bad advice to teenagers,

People said it didn't matter.

When he appointed Mark Lloyd as diversity czar and he believed in curtailing free speech, taking from one and giving to another to spread the wealth and admires Hugo Chavez,

People said it didn't matter.

When Valerie Jarrett was selected as Obama's senior White House advisor and she is an avowed Socialist,

People said it didn't matter.

When Anita Dunn, White House Communications director said Mao Tse Tung was her favorite philosopher and the person she turned to most for inspiration,

People said it didn't matter.

When he appointed Carol Browner as global warming czar, and she is a well known socialist working on Cap and trade as the nations largest tax,

People said it doesn't matter.

When he appointed Van Jones, an ex-con and avowed Communist as green energy czar, who since had to resign when this was made known,

People said it didn't matter.

When Tom Daschle, Obama's pick for health and human services secretary could not be confirmed, because he was a tax cheat,

People said it didn't matter.

When as president of the United States, he bowed to the King of Saudi Arabia ,

People said it didn't matter.

When he traveled around the world criticizing America and never once talking of her greatness,

People said it didn't matter.

When his actions concerning the middle-
east seemed to support the Palestinians over Israel, our long time friend,
People said it doesn't matter.

When he upset the Europeans by remov-
ing plans for a missile defense system
against the Russians,
People said it doesn't matter.

When he played politics in Afghanistan
by not sending troops the Field Com-
manders said we had to have to win,
People said it didn't matter.

When he started spending us into a debt
that was so big we could not pay it off,
People said it didn't matter.

When he took a huge spending bill under
the guise of stimulus and used it to pay off
organizations, unions and individuals that
got him elected,
People said it didn't matter.

When he took over insurance companies, car companies, banks, etc.

People said it didn't matter.

When he took away student loans from the banks and put it through the government,

People said it didn't matter.

When he designed plans to take over the health care system and put it under government control,

People said it didn't matter.

When he set into motion a plan to take over the control of all energy in the United States through Cap and Trade,

People said it didn't matter.

When he finally completed his transformation of America into a Socialist State,

People finally woke up........ but it was too late.

Ron Berger 182

Any one of these things, in and of themselves does not really matter. But.... when you add them up one by one you get a phenomenal score that points to the fact that our Obama is determined to make America over into a Marxist/Socialist society. All of the items in the preceding paragraphs have been put into place. All can be documented very easily. Before you disavow this, do an internet search. The last paragraph alone is not yet cast in stone. You and I will write that paragraph. Will it read as above or will it be a more happy ending for most of America? Personally, I like happy endings.

If you are an Obama Supporter, please do not be angry with me because I think your president is a socialist. There are too many facts supporting this. If you seek the truth you will be richer for it. Don't just belittle the opposition. Search for the truth. I did. Democrats, Republicans, Independents, Constitutionalist, Libertarians and what have you, we all need to pull together. We all must pull together or watch the demise of a society that we all love and cherish. If you are a religious person, pray for our nation.

Never before in the history of America have we been confronted with problems so huge that the very existence of our country is in jeopardy. Don't rely on most television news and what you read in the newspapers for the truth. Search the internet. Yes, there is a lot of bad information, lies and distortions there too but you are smart enough to spot the fallacies. Newspapers are a dying breed. They are currently seeking a bailout from the government. Do you really think they are about to print the truth? Obama praises all the television news networks except Fox who he has waged war against. There must be a reason. He does not call them down on any specifics, just a general battle against them. If they lie, he should call them out on it but he doesn't. Find the truth, it will set you free.

Our biggest enemy is not China, Russia, or Iran; no, our biggest enemy is a contingent of politicians in Washington DC.

****

**

Dr. David Barton is more of a historian than a Biblical speaker, but very famous for his knowledge of historical facts as well as Biblical truths.

Dr. David Barton - on Obama

Respect the Office? Yes.

Respect the Man in the Office? No, I am sorry to say.

I have noted that many elected officials, both Democrats and Republicans, called upon America to unite behind Obama.

Well, I want to make it clear to all who will listen that I AM NOT uniting behind Obama!

I will respect the Office which he holds, and I will acknowledge his abilities as an orator and wordsmith, BUT that is it.

I have begun today to see what I can do to make sure that he is a one-term President!

Why am I doing this?

It is because:

 - I do not share Obama's vision or value system for America;

 - I do not share his Abortion beliefs;

- I do not share his radical Marxist's concept of re-distributing wealth;

- I do not share his stated views on raising taxes on those who make $150,000+ (the ceiling has been changed three times since August);

- I do not share his view that America is Arrogant;

- I do not share his view that America is not a Christian Nation;

- I do not share his view that the military should be reduced by 25%;

- I do not share his view of amnesty and giving more to illegal's than our American Citizens who need help;

- I do not share his views on homosexuality and his definition of marriage;

- I do not share his views that Radical Islam is our friend and Israel is our enemy who should give up any land;

- I do not share his spiritual beliefs (at least the ones he has made public);

- I do not share his beliefs on how to re-work the healthcare system in America;

- I do not share his Strategic views of the Middle East; and

- I certainly do not share his plan to sit down with terrorist regimes such as Iran.

Bottom line: my America is vastly different from Obama's, and I have a higher obligation to my Country and my GOD to do what is Right!

For eight (8) years, the Liberals in our Society, led by numerous entertainers who would have no platform and no real credibility but for their celebrity status, have attacked President Bush, his family, and his spiritual beliefs!

They have not moved toward the center in their beliefs and their philosophies, and they never came together nor compromised their personal beliefs for the betterment of our Country!

They have portrayed my America as a land where everything is tolerated except being intolerant!

They have been a vocal and irreverent minority for years!

They have mocked and attacked the very core values so important to the founding and growth of our Country!

They have made every effort to remove the name of GOD or Jesus Christ from our Society!

They have challenged capital punishment, the right to bear firearms, and the most basic principles of our criminal code!

They have attacked one of the most fundamental of all Freedoms, the right of free speech!

Unite behind Obama? Never ! ! !

I am sure many of you who read this think that I am going overboard, but I refuse to retreat one more inch in favor of those whom I believe are the embodiment of Evil!

PRESIDENT BUSH made many mistakes during his Presidency, and I am not sure how history will judge him. However, I believe that he weighed his decisions in light of the long established Judeo-Christian principles of our Founding Fathers!!!

Majority rules in America , and I will honor the concept; however, I will fight with all of my power to be a voice in opposition to Obama and his "goals for America ."

I am going to be a thorn in the side of those who, if left unchecked, will destroy our Country!! Any more compromise is more defeat!

I pray that the results of the next election will wake up many who have sat on the sidelines and allowed the Socialist-Marxist anti-GOD crowd to slowly change so much of what has been good in America ! "Error of Opinion may be tolerated where Reason is left free to combat it." - Thomas Jefferson

GOD bless you and GOD bless our Country!!!

Thanks for your time, be safe. "In GOD We Trust"

"If we ever forget that we're one nation under GOD, then we will be a nation gone under." - Ronald Reagan

I WANT THE AMERICA I GREW UP IN BACK....

In GOD We Trust........

I agree with Dr. David Barton.

****

Many times you think things are going one way and then you find out some deep and dark secrets that just never entered your mind. When the government bailed out GM and Chrysler you would think it was just a transfer of funds which would be paid back, with interest, at some time in the future. However, the following tells a story about the small print that just never seems to surface.

**

Does it surprise you????? I do not think that anything will come of it...

Chrysler--A Very Dirty Story

Sooner or later it will all come to light!

This could be a scandal of epic proportions and one that makes Nixon's Watergate or Clinton 's Monica Lewinsky affair pale by comparison. Why was there neither rhyme nor reason as to which dealerships of the Chrysler Corporation were to be closed?

Roll the clock back to the weeks just before Chrysler declared bankruptcy. Chrysler, like GM, was in dire financial straits and federal government "graciously" offered to "buy the company" and keep them out of bankruptcy and "save jobs."

Chrysler was, in the words of Obama and his administration, "Too big to fail," same story with GM. The feds organized their "Automotive Task Force" to fix Chrysler and GM. Obama, in an act that is 100% unconstitutional, appointed a guy named Steve Rattner to be the White House's official Car Czar - literally, that's what his title is.

Rattner is the liaison between Obama, Chrysler, and GM. Initially, the national media reported that Chrysler 'had made this list of dealerships'. Not true! The Washington Examiner, Newsmax, Fox News and a host of other news agencies discovered that the list of dealerships was put together by the "Automotive Task Force" headed by no one other than Mr. Steve Rattner.

Now the plot thickens.

Remember earlier we said that there was neither rhyme nor reason why certain dealerships were closed?

Actually there's a very interesting pattern as to who was closed down. Again, on

May 27, 2009, The Washington Examiner and Newsmax exposed the connection.

Amazingly, of the 789 dealerships closed by the federal government, 788 had donated money, exclusively to Republican political causes, while contributing nothing to Democratic political causes. The only "Democratic" dealership on the list was found to have donated $7,700 to Hillary's campaign, and a bit over $2,000 to John Edwards. The same dealership, reportedly, also gave $200.00 to Obama's campaign. Does that seem a little odd to you?

Steve Rattner is the guy who put the list together. Well, he happens to be married to a Maureen White. Maureen happens to be the former national finance chairman of the Democratic National Committee. As such, she has access to campaign donation records from everyone in the nation- Republican or Democrat. But of course, this is just a wacky "coincidence," we're certain.

Then comes another really wacky "coincidence."

On that list of dealerships being closed down, a weird thing happened in Arkansas , North Louisiana, and Southern Missouri . It seems that Bill Clinton's former White House Chief of Staff, Mack McClarty, owns a chain of dealership in that region, partnered with a fellow by the name of Robert Johnson. Johnson happens to be founder of Black Entertainment Television and was a huge Obama supporter and financier. These guys own a half dozen Chrysler stores under the company title of RLJ-McClarty-Landers. Interestingly, none of their dealerships were ordered closed - not one! While all of their competing Chrysler/ Dodge and Jeep dealership were! Eight dealerships located near the dealerships owned by McClarty and Johnson were ordered shut down. Thus by pure luck, these two major Obama supporters now have virtual monopoly on Chrysler sales in their zone.

Isn't that amazing?

Go look in The Washington Examiner, the story's there, and it's in a dozen or so other web-based news organizations; this isn't being made up.

Now if you thought Chrysler was owned by Fiat, you are mistaken. Under the federal court ruling, 65% of Chrysler is now owned by the federal government and the United Auto Workers union! Fiat owns 20%. The other 15% is still privately owned and presumably will be traded on the stock market. Obama smiles and says he doesn't want to run the auto industry.

As horrifying as this is to comprehend, and being as how this used to be the United States of America , it would appear that the president has the power to destroy private businesses and eliminate upwards of 100,000 jobs just because they don't agree with his political agenda. This is Nazi Germany stuff, and it's happening right here, right now, in our back yard.

There are voices in Washington demanding an explanation, but the "Automotive Task Force" has released no information to the public or to any of the senators demanding answers for what has been done. Keep your ear to the ground for more on this story. If you've ever wanted to make a difference about anything in your life, get on the phone to your national senator or representative in the House and demand an investigation into this. Benjamin Franklin had it right when he said, "All that's necessary for evil to triumph is for good men to do nothing." Car Czar No More

An amazing thing happened as this story was going to press.Obama's Car Czar, Steve Rattner, resigned on July 13 and was promptly replaced by former steel workers union boss Ron Bloom. According to CBS News, Rattner left "to return to private life and spend time with his family." Treasury Secretary Tim Geithner said, "I hope that he takes another opportunity to bring his unique skills to government service in the future."

By the way, Rattner is under investigation for a multi-million dollar pay-to-play investment bank scandal in New York ....

Uh-oh!

But, we're certain that had nothing to do with his resignation.

And, according to several news sources out there, there are rumors he's being investigated for what could be pay-to-play scandal involving the closing of Chrysler and GM dealerships. Really? Again, that couldn't have anything to with his resignation-that's ridiculous! Like CBS said, this guy just wants to "spend more quality time with his family."

Obama has 32 personally appointed "czars" who answer to no one but him, all of whom are acting without any Constitutional authority. But hey, we're sure they all have "unique skills,"......as Tim Geithner likes to say!

SOOOOO.HOWS THE CHANGE WORKING FOR YOU?..

Check it out at the following websites.....

http://www.washingtonexaminer.com/opinion/blogs/beltway-confidential/Furor-grows-over-partisan-car-dealer-closings-46261447.html

< http://www.washingtonexaminer.com/politics/Obamas-auto-policy-All-in-the-Democratic-family-44414452.html >http://www.washingtonexaminer.com/politics/Obamas-auto-policy-All-in-the-Democratic-family-44414452.html

This goes beyond corruption in high places - to gross criminal actions on the part of our government! I hope you will spread this far and wide, and hopefully the taxpaying public will demand some of that transparency we were promised......followed by criminal prosecution of the perpetrators!

What a crooked government, we have!!!!! Vote 'em all out...November, 2010!

****

There are other stories that will rock you. BO and his "henchmen" are hard at work trying to make sure that they buy enough votes during this time to carry over to 2012.

**

Oklahoma Governor Brad Henry announces that the Obama administration rejected his request for disaster assistance, following record floods in the state and a declared state of emergency. Koco.com states, "The White House gave no reason for denying the disaster aid request." (In the 2008 presidential election Senator John McCain defeated Obama in Oklahoma 64–34 percent. Obama also ignored Tennessee after record flooding in May—the worst disaster in the state's history; McCain defeated Obama in that state 57–42 percent.)

Probably the reason Arizona is being treated 'rotten' by the president is because it was McCain's state and still is.

****

There have been calls for BO to resign, but the word just doesn't filter down to him. The "evil ones" have a big hold on the USA and they wont give it up without a fight. You can bet that every dirty trick in the book will be played before the next presidential election.

**

Should Pres. Obama Resign Over Feb. 13?

By Kevin McCullough

While defending his own policies President Obama has routinely been rude and sarcastic to his predecessor, George W. Bush. Yet Obama appears to be making the resident of the previous White House look like a genius compared to his own serious missteps in office.

Case in point ^ Interior Secretary Ken Salazar's performance and the communication of priorities on the issue of oil rig safety in the Gulf of Mexico.

It seems incomprehensible that the president and other members of the administration still have jobs when it is now being reported that the federal government was apprised by BP on February 13 that the Deepwater Horizon oil rig was leaking oil and natural gas into the ocean floor.

In fact, according to documents in the administration's possession, BP was fighting large cracks at the base of the well for roughly ten days in early February.

Further it seems the administration was also informed about this development, six weeks before to the rig's fatal explosion when an engineer from the University of California, Berkeley, announced to the world a near miss of an explosion on the rig by stating, "They damn near blew up the rig."

It's also now being reported that BP was asking for the administration's help on this matter long before the deadly accident and the now gushing well of tar.

Which leads me to some questions for the president. If I were in front row of reporters in the White House briefing room, here's what I'd like to know:

1. It appears, Mr. President, that you were informed by BP about problems on Deepwater Horizon on February 13 and the company wanted your help. What did you say?

2. Given this new revelation,   Mr. President, how can you can sleep at night knowing that your inaction cost the lives of eleven men in Louisiana?

3, Did you inform the victims' families about these facts when you invited them to the White House for last month's photo op?

4. You've said, Mr. President, time and again, that the buck stops with you. Doesn't that statement seem like something bordering on propaganda when you follow it up with what appears to be a false sense of outrage by telling Matt Lauer that you're looking for rear ends to kick?

5. Does the buck stop with you or not?

6. Are you going to insist that Mr. Salazar step down from his post in disgrace and shame?

7. Will you hold another prime time television press conference and tell the entire truth to the American people? -- These would be the actions of a man who says that the buck stops" with him.

8. I know when this news was breaking midday on Saturday about the latest BP

developments that you and the Vice President were out on the golf course. Was it 39th or 40th time you've played a round in 18 months? (Just for a point of reference President Bush played golf 24 times in eight years.) Never mind, your priorities are for you to decide. At least until election night...

And now here's where I would not be able to stop myself from saying more...

It is one thing, Mr. President, to be forced to deal with unexpected circumstances and to have to deal with genuinely new problems. President Bush sure had to. He had to respond to an attack on our homeland that took the lives of 3,000 of our fellow citizens. But on his watch no other terrorist actions took lives of Americans on our soil, largely due to his steadfast leadership and willingness to accept no excuses on the matter.

But Mr. President, you seem to have very little leadership experience and it appears you have even less skill. Being a good dad and nice guy who sees the world as he wishes it to be is not exactly a resume of exacting leadership.

Your advisers have failed you and you have failed the American people on nearly everything we've asked of you.

Where you go from here is really your call, but you should consider two options if you genuinely love the country you work for and those of us you report to.

First, change your tactics. Second, appear to care. Attempt to engage and empower Americans who can and will go solve this mess.

Otherwise resign.

For the good of the nation, for your own children's future, change your patterns or change your path... but change!

You do remember that word don't you, Mr. President?

****

While we're on the subject of dirty tricks - please read the following:

**

How the Government Slowed Down the Gulf Cleanup

Tuesday, 22 Jun 2010 03:31 PM

By: Ernest Istook

Our own government has quietly admitted that America needs foreign help to handle the oil spill almost two months after pushing that help away.

Far more oil could have been intercepted before it fouled the Gulf Coast. So why hasn't our government apologized?

By refusing foreign assistance, we banned both the latest technology and cleanup vessels that far exceed the capacity of America's oil spill response vessels (OSRVs). We rejected ships with 10 times the capability of the vessels we used instead.

In a quiet announcement on June 18, the Federal On-Scene Coordinator (FOSC) finally agreed that we need help, describing a conclusion reached two days before:

. . . the FOSC, in coordination with other federal agencies, determined on June 16,

2010, pursuant to 46 U.S.C. §55113, that there are an insufficient number of specialized oil skimming vessels in the U.S. to keep pace with the unprecedented levels of oil discharges in the Gulf of Mexico. Based upon this determination, foreign specialized skimming vessels may be deployed to response operations.

Technically, the Jones Act remains unwaived and continues to restrict use of foreign vessels other than OSRV's. Officials invoked only a limited exemption that was put into law after Hurricane Katrina.

By their delay, our bureaucracy and government regulation have made a horrible situation even worse. There were two weeks between the April 20 explosion on the Deepwater Horizon and the time when the first oil made landfall. And it was almost six additional weeks before specialized equipment from overseas was approved by our government for limited use.

The Dutch formally offered help on April 25. Not until June 14 did the U.S. State Department announce that some foreign help would be welcomed from the 17 nations who had been trying to assist.

We violated a basic rule of oil spills: The key to avoiding catastrophic damage and extreme liability is a fast response.

So what's different about the foreign equipment that at long last is being deployed? Capacity, for one. They can do far more and do it more quickly.

To protect the North Sea - a major petroleum-producing area - Europe created cooperatives such as Norway's Norwegian Clean Seas Association for Operating Companies (NOFO), assembling resources that far surpass America's.

The largest American OSRV I've found has only a 4,000-barrel capacity. Compare that to Norway's new cleanup standards, which state, "An active effort must always be made to achieve the largest possible tank capacity. Under no circumstances must the tank capacity for storage of recovered oil be less than 1,500 m". 1,500 cubic meters is 9,400 barrels. None of our U.S. oil recovery vessels appear to come even close to this standard.

The European Union maintains a multi-faceted inventory of OSRVs. The Netherlands alone lists 11 ships that exceed this 9,400-barrel capacity, including vessels like the Geopotes 14 that reportedly can pick up and contain 47,000 barrels at a time. That's 10 times larger than any U.S. ship we've been using.

Collecting more oil in each run enables more time spent collecting oil and less time carrying oil back to a storage facility.

There's another problem with how U.S. regulations are slowing down the cleanup. The Dutch are now providing skimmers that can be attached to American vessels. But because most of what's skimmed is unavoidably water, not oil, they complain that America's EPA standards won't let them put back the water. Thus their tanks fill up with a mixture that is mostly water.

That mix is a serious problem. The Incident Commander, Coast Guard Admiral Thad Allen, told the media on June 11, "We have skimmed, to date, about 18 million gallons of oily water ~ the oil has to be decanted from that [and] our yield is usually somewhere around 10 percent or 15 percent on that.

That means 85 percent to 90 percent of what is collected is water, not oil. If complaints are correct, then unless vessels can separate these at sea and discharge the water, most of what they haul back to a storage facility is water. That means six or seven trips to carry one full load of skimmed oil. Complaints are that our EPA says discharged water from the skimming cannot exceed 15 ppm (parts per million) of oil.

Radio Netherlands reported:

"The Americans don't have spill response vessels with skimmers because their environment regulations do not allow it. With the Dutch method, seawater is sucked up with the oil by the skimmer. The oil is stored in the tanker and the superfluous water is pumped overboard. But the water does contain some oil residue, and that is too much according to U.S. environment regulations.

Wierd Koops [head of the Dutch consortium, Spill Response Group Holland] thinks the U.S. approach is nonsense, because otherwise you would have to store the surplus seawater in the tanks as well.

[Says Koops], "We say no, you have to get as much oil as possible into the storage tanks and as little water as possible. So we pump the water, which contains drops of oil, back overboard.

U.S. regulations are contradictory, Mr. Koops stresses. Pumping water back into the sea with oil residue is not allowed.

He is not alone in criticizing America's restrictions on the cleanup efforts. Several Democrats in Congress have joined the calls to get our bureaucracy out of the way.

Rep. Corinne Brown, D-Fla., said at a hearing, "We are in emergency mode; we need skimmers . . . There are small boats, I guess, but we need the big ones. I understand they are available in other countries."

We indeed need the big cleanup ships that America must get from overseas. Who knows how many livelihoods and how much of the environment would have been spared if our government had not drug its bureaucratic feet and invited them two months ago?

BP has apologized. And still must be held accountable. But where's the apology from our government - and the accountability?

Ernest Istook served 14 years as a U.S. congressman and is now a distinguished fellow at The Heritage Foundation.

****

    I hope that reading all these emails, so far, really churns up your anger and you start to voice your opinions.

    I really believe that the large number of complaining emails that I receive is very representative of the country's true feelings. I truly am indebted to all those that have sent me this information with the hope that I could do something with it. Maybe I can lend a hand in getting this message out to the public in general.

I am not a racist, agitator or mentally deranged in any way (I hope) but, I am totally PO'd at how our liberties, constitution, Bill of Rights, way of life, reputation, and military are being trampled on. This administration can only claim one thing and that is to be the first elected black man to this post. Everything else has been a bushel of lies from the very start.

The one promise BO is keeping is that he said he wanted change and the voters agreed. But, they just didn't fathom the kind of change he meant. This change is leading us down the path to bankruptcy and all BO can think about is spending more and then increasing the taxes to pay for it.

Already the government owns two automobile makers, many financial institutions and a number of businesses. Even though much of this has never been tried before by the government, they will all fail if the government continues in control. Everything the government has touched, with the purpose of "controlling" has failed or gone broke. I just seems like these liberals have no idea of how to run a business and they are led by a person who has absolutely no experience in ANY-THING.

THE SHADY BUNCH

One Candle at a Time

| GOVERNMENT CAN FIX HEALTH CARE. | JUST LOOK AT MEDICARE AND MEDICAID. | OKAY, THEY'RE BROKE, BUT LOOK AT SOCIAL SECURITY. | OKAY, IT'S BROKE, BUT LOOK AT THE U.S. POST OFFICE. |
| OKAY, IT'S BROKE, BUT LOOK AT AMTRAK. | OKAY, IT'S BROKE, BUT LOOK AT FANNIE MAE AND FREDDIE MAC. | OKAY, THEY'RE BROKE, BUT LOOK AT MY BUDGET. | OKAY, IT'S $1.6 TRILLION IN THE RED, BUT.... |

This has got to be the best quote of the year

"As an American I am not so shocked that Obama was given the Nobel Peace Prize

Ron Berger 213

without any accomplishments to his name, but that America gave him the White House based on the same credentials."

Newt Gingrich

BO even has the Nobel Prize people fooled. Can you imagine someone getting this award for what is meant to be for an accomplishment filled life or outstanding achievement and given to someone who has reached none of these goals? It certainly sheds doubt on those that really deserve it.

What were the requirements needed to qualify for this award? If someone has done NOTHING in his life - how can he possibly be in the running - and then win?

Just another example that the world is going to hell in a hand basket. Is there no justice left in the world or are those "judges" wanting to get in good with the "great one" or as he likes to be called - "I am the one"?

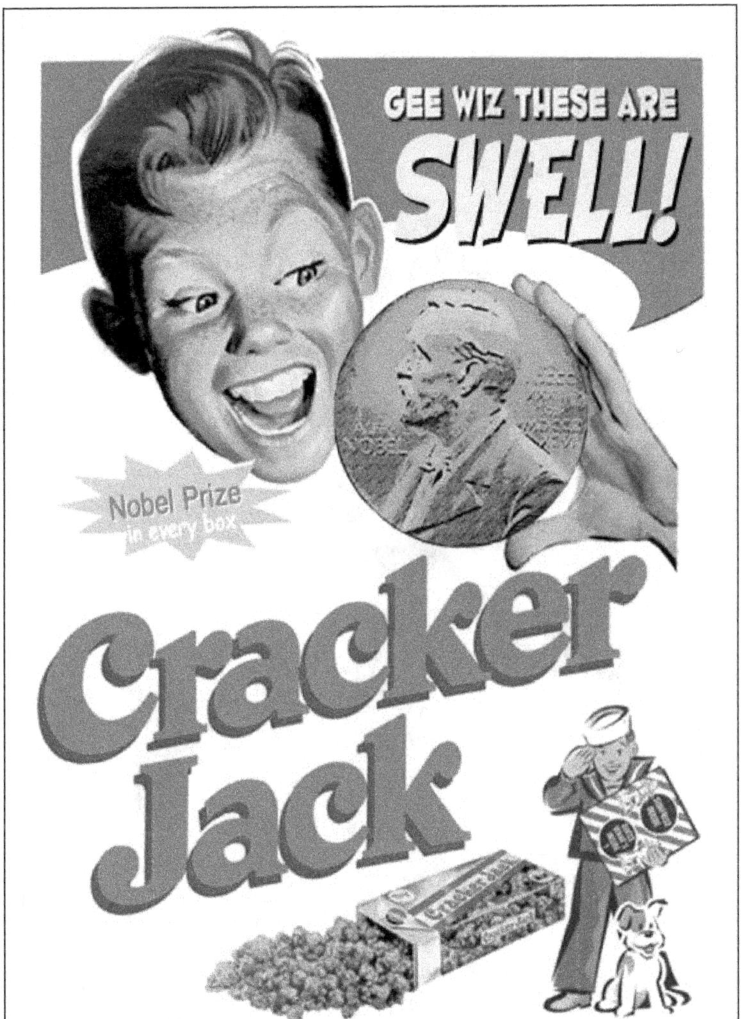
GEE WIZ THESE ARE
SWELL!
Nobel Prize
in every box
Cracker
Jack
Candy-Coated Popcorn, Peanuts, and a Nobel Peace Prize...
That's What You Get In Cracker Jack!
Maksim-ThePeoplesCube.com

One Candle at a Time

These comics may make you chuckle, but they certainly depict reality. How can anyone not see that these point to his fallibility? He is a <u>nothing</u> that talked his way into the presidency. Even the high and mighty Kennedy backed him up. It's too bad that he isn't alive now to see what BO has turned into. Then, again, Ted probably wouldn't see BO in this light. He'd play politics and claim that he was doing a great job.

The time has come to take out the trash. November 2, 2010 is "trash day" and it's the first day of our redemption. Our first step in cleaning up the mess in Washington. We need to send enough conservatives back to DC to do some good. Once that is accomplished, we can work on 2012.

**

And it came to pass in the Age of Insanity that the people of the land Called America, having lost their morals, their initiative, and their Will to defend their liberties, chose as their Supreme Leader that Person known as "The One.." He emerged from the vapors with a message that had no meaning; but He Hypnotized the people telling them, "I am sent to save you." My lack Of experience, my questionable ethics, my monstrous ego, and my Association with evil doers are of no consequence. I shall save you With hope and Change. Go, therefore, and proclaim throughout the Land that he who proceeded me is evil, that he has defiled the nation, And that all he has built must be destroyed. And the people rejoiced, For even though they knew not what "The One" would do, he had promised That it was good; and they believed. And "The One" said " We live in The greatest country in the world. Help me change everything about it!" And the people said, "Hallelujah! Change is good!"

Ron Berger 218

Then He said, "We are going to tax the rich fat-cats." And the People said "Sock it to them!" "And redistribute their wealth." And The people said, "Show us the money!" And then he said, "Redistribution of wealth is good for everybody."

And Joe the plumber asked, "Are you kidding me? You're going to steal my money and give it to the deadbeats??" And "The One" ridiculed and taunted him, and Joe's personal records were hacked and publicized. One lone reporter asked, "Isn't that Marxist policy?" And she was banished from the kingdom!

Then a citizen asked, "With no foreign relations experience and having zero military experience or knowledge, how will you deal with radical terrorists?" And "The One" said, "Simple. I shall sit with them and talk with them and show them how nice we really are; and they will forget that they ever wanted to kill us al!" And the people said, "Hallelujah!! We are safe at last, and we can beat our weapons Into free cars for the people!"

Then "The One" said "I shall give 95% of you lower taxes." And one, Lone voice said, "But 40% of us don't pay ANY taxes." So "The One" said, "Then I shall give you some of the taxes the fat-cats pay!" And the people said, "Hallelujah! Show us the money!" Then "The One" said, "I shall tax your Capital Gains when you sell your homes!" And the people yawned and the slumping housing market collapsed. And He said. "I shall mandate employer-funded health care for every worker and raise the minimum wage. And I shall give every person unlimited healthcare and medicine and transportation to the clinics." And the people said, "Give me some of that!" Then he said, "I shall penalize employers who ship jobs overseas." And the people said, "Where's my rebate check?"

Then "The One" said, "I shall bankrupt the coal industry and electricity rates will sky-rocket!" And the people said, "Coal is Dirty, coal is evil, no more coal! But we don't care for that part about higher electric rates." So "The One" said, not to worry. If your rebate isn't enough to cover your expenses, we shall bail you out. Just sign up with the ACORN and you troubles are over!"

Then he said, "Illegal immigrants feel scorned and slighted. Let's grant them amnesty, Social Security, free education, free lunches, free medical care, bi-lingual signs and guaranteed housing...." And The people said, "Hallelujah!" and they made him king!

And so it came to pass that employers, facing spiraling costs and ever-higher taxes, raised their prices and laid off workers. Others simply gave up and went out of business and the economy sank like unto a rock dropped from a cliff. The banking industry was destroyed. Manufacturing slowed to a crawl. And more of the people were without a means of support.

Then "The One" said, "I am the "the One"- The Messiah - and I'm here to save you! We shall just print more money so everyone will have enough!" But our foreign trading partners said unto Him. "Wait a minute. Your dollar is not worth a pile of camel dung! You will have to pay more... And "The One" said, "Wait a minute. That is unfair!!" And the world said, "Neither are these other idiotic programs you have embraced. Lo, you have become a Socialist state and a second-rate power. Now you shall play by our rules!"

And the people cried out, "Alas, alas!! What have we done?" But yea verily, it was too late. The people set upon The One and spat upon him and stoned him, and his name was dung. And the once mighty nation was no more; and the once proud people were without sustenance or shelter or hope. And the change "The One" had given them was as like unto a poison that had destroyed them and like a whirlwind that consumed all that they had built.

And the people beat their chests in despair and cried out in anguish, "give us back our nation and our pride and our hope!!" But it was too late, and their homeland was no more.

Ron Berger 222

You may think this a fairy tale, but it's not. It's happening RIGHT NOW.

THIS really tells it like it is. After reading it -- and before you go into the bathroom to throw-up -- forward it to your friends and those you know who care about our country and what is happening to it under the rule of Commissar Obamanation.

P.S. --Yeah, this is too true to be funny. Tragic, but not funny; tragic but true.

****

I want to present some emails that really show how much of leader BO really is:

**

In 1952, President Truman established one day a year as a National Day of Prayer.

In 1988, President Reagan designated the first Thursday in May of each year as the National Day of Prayer.

In June 2007, (then) Presidential candidate Barack Obama declared that the USA was no longer a Christian nation.

This year President Obama, canceled the 21st annual National Day of Prayer ceremony at the White House under the ruse of "not wanting to offend anyone".

On September 25, 2009 from 4 am until 7 PM, a National Day of Prayer for the Muslim religion was held on Capitol Hill, beside the White House. There were over 50,000 Muslims that day in DC.

I guess it doesn't matter if "Christians" are offended by this event - we obviously don't count as "anyone" anymore.

The direction this country is headed should strike fear in the heart of every Christian. Especially knowing that the Muslim religion believes that if Christians cannot be converted they should be annihilated

This is not a rumor - Go to the web site to confirm this info:

www.islamoncapitolhill.com <http://www.islamoncapitolhill.com_/> (http://www.islamoncapitolhill.com/)

Please pass this on, maybe someone, somehow can figure out a way to put

America back on the map as it was when we were growing up, a safe place to live and by the Ten Commandments and Pledge of Allegiance, etc!

****

**

Dear Fellow Conservative, Americans & Friends,

This has got to be the epitome of arrogance. Pass this on to all your friends, etc, etc, etc so all of America can know what type of man was voted it by the liberals. Let's get him out.

THIS HAS GOT TO BE THE MOST OUTRAGEOUS STATEMENT EVER MADE BY A PUBLIC OFFICIAL LET ALONE BY THE PRESIDENT OF THE UNITED STATES.. AND THIS GUY IS OUR "COMMANDER IN CHIEF".

HERE IS HIS RESPONSE WHEN HE BACKED OFF FROM HIS DECISION TO REQUIRE THE MILITARY PAY FOR THEIR WAR INJURIES.

Bad press, including major mockery of the plan by comedian Jon Stewart, led to President Obama abandoning his proposal to require veterans carry private health insurance to cover the estimated $540 million annual cost to the federal government of treatment for

injuries to military personnel received during their tours on active duty. The President admitted that he was puzzled by the magnitude of the opposition to his proposal.

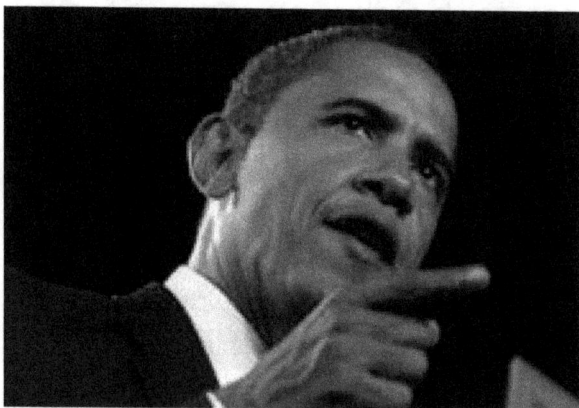

"Look, it's an all volunteer force," Obama complained. "Nobody made these guys go to war. They had to have known and accepted the risks. Now they whine about bearing the costs of their choice? It doesn't compute.." "I thought these were people who were proud to sacrifice for their country, "Obama continued "I wasn't asking for blood, just money. With the country facing the worst financial crisis in its history, I'd have thought that the patriotic thing to do would be to try to help reduce the nation's deficit.

I guess I underestimated the selfishness of some of my fellow Americans."

Please pass this on to every one including every vet and their families whom you know. How in the world did a person with this mindset become our leader?

REMEMBER THIS STATEMENT...

"Nobody made these guys go to war.

They had to have known and accepted the risks.

 Now they whine about bearing the costs of their choice?"

If he thinks he will ever get another vote from an Active Duty, Reserve, National Guard service member or veteran of a military service he ought to think it over. If you or a family member is or has served their country please pass this to them.

Please pass this to everyone.

I'm guessing that other than the 20-25 percent hardcore liberals in the US will agree that this is just another example why <u>this is the worst president in American history</u>. Remind everyone over and over how this man thinks, while he bows to the Saudi Arabian king.

****

Ron Berger 228

**

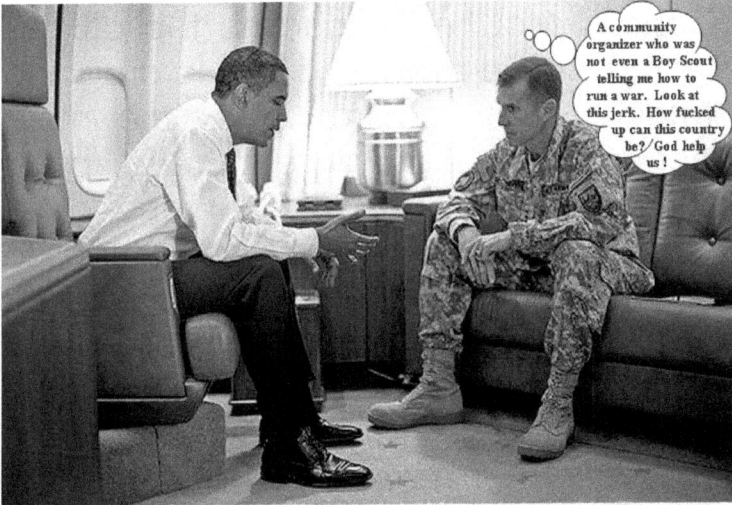

Obama: "Listen Stan, just because you graduated from West Point, have 33 years military experience and real leadership abilities, became a 4 Star General making life and death decisions daily doesn't' mean you know anything about how to fight a war and defeat an enemy. So, just do what I say. OK".

****

This one really takes the cake. BO is telling General Stan McChrystal how to fight the war in Afghanistan. He also fired the General for telling the truth.

**

Follow up comments from the General & Community Organizer -

Quote by Paul R. Hollrah:

"General McChrystal and his top officers are not simple-minded, knuckle-dragging brutes. To the contrary, they are intelligent, thoughtful, highly educated, patriots...graduates of West Point and other fine universities...who are dedicated to duty, honor, and country. To think that such men would be so careless as to speak unflatteringly of Obama, Biden, and other top administration figures, in the presence of a reporter for a notoriously left wing publication, defies logic...at the very least. To think that men who are trained to be careful and deliberate in everything they do, could do something so careless and so unguarded is simply beyond comprehension. I would argue that McChrystal and his aides knew exactly what they were doing.

What is now lost in all of the hand-wringing and speculation is the fact that General McChrystal and his people have succeeded in doing exactly what they set out to do. They wanted to plant the seed in the minds of the American people that

Obama is not up to the task of being Commander in Chief and that he does not command the respect of the men and women of the uniformed services...from the newest Private E-1 up to the top four-star generals and admirals.

That seed is now firmly planted and it cannot be unplanted.

From this day forward, no one will have to tell the American people that General Stanley McChrystal is a true warrior, a man's man, and that Barack Obama is nothing more than a...community organizer. Well done, General!"

My Comments: Billy in VA

Everyone should know that not only the Secretary of Defense during the Vietnam War, but arguably the smartest General of the time knew that the War was not worth the sacrifices our country was experiencing; however, they chose not to say a word until the war was over.

Although the low life bastard, Robert McNamara, was a prime architect of the Vietnam War and repeatedly overruled the Joint Chief of Staff (JCS) on strategic matters, McNamara was skeptical about whether the war could be won, A CLAIM HE WOULD PUBLISH IN HIS BOOK YEARS LATER. McNamara must have known about the deadly effects of Agent Orange, Purple, and other deadly chemicals, even as it was being used in Vietnam, and long before veterans came home to die or waste away from the herbicide's after-effects. He must have been involved in the decision to use Agent Orange. This piece of crap, Robert McNamara, directly caused the loss of lives of over 58,000 US Military personnel and should have been jailed for life.

General Frederick Weyand told a reporter that the Vietnam War was not winnable. Can you imagine how many lives could have been saved if General Weyand had made his assessment known early in the war (maybe over 50,000, not to mention those hundreds of thousands that were severely wounded in body and mind). General Weyand was the last commander of American military operations in the Vietnam War from 1972–1973, and served as the 28th US Army Chief of Staff from 1974-1976.

AT LEAST GENERAL McCHRYSTAL AND HIS STAFF DIDN'T WAIT...THEY GOT THE WORD OUT NOW! HOO-AH for General McChrystal and his patriots at staff.

****

MARINE CORPS

What's your major malfunction numbnuts?
You're a Harvard grad and don't know the
difference between CORPS and CORPSE?
You flunked lunch at Harvard, didn't you?

Here are some other brilliant decisions by BO:

**

HB 1388 PASSED..!!

You just spent $20,000,000 to move members/supporters of Hamas, a terrorist organization, to the United States; housing, food, the whole enchilada.

HB-1388 PASSED

Whether you are an Obama fan, or not, EVERYONE IN THE U.S. needs to know.....

Something happened... H.R. 1388 was passed, behind our backs.

You may want to read about it... It wasn't mentioned on the news... just went by on the ticker tape at the bottom of the CNN screen.

Obama funds $20M in tax payer dollars to immigrate Hamas Refugees to the USA.

This is the news that didn't make the headlines....

By executive order, President Barack Obama has ordered the expenditure of $20.3 million in "migration assistance" to the Palestinian refugees and "conflict victims" in Gaza ..

The "presidential determination," which allows hundreds of thousands of Palestinians with ties to Hamas to resettle in the United States, was signed and appears in the Federal Register.

Few on Capitol Hill, or in the media, took note that the order provides a free ticket replete with housing and food allowances to individuals who have displayed their overwhelming support to the Islamic Resistance Movement (Hamas) in the parliamentary election of January 2006.

Let's review....itemized list of some of Barack Obama's most recent actions since his inauguration:

His first call to any head of state, as president, was to Mahmoud Abbas, leader of Fatah party in the Palestinian territory.

His first one-on-one television interview with any news organization was with Al Arabia television.

His first executive order was to fund/facilitate abortion(s) not just here within the U. S. but throughout the world, using U.S. tax payer funds.

He ordered Guantanamo Bay closed and all military trials of detainees halted.

He ordered overseas CIA interrogation centers closed.

He withdrew all charges against the masterminds behind the USS Cole and the "terror attack" on 9/11.

Now we learn that he is allowing hun-dreds of thousands of Palestinian refuges to move to, and live in, the US at American taxpayer expense.

These important, and insightful, issues are being "lost" in the blinding bail-outs and "stimulation" packages.

Doubtful? To verify this for yourself:

www.thefederalregister.com/d.p/2009-02-04-E9-2488 <;

****

The question of BO's birth certificate is still an issue. It really is hard to fathom that the modern press can't find the facts. The following email tells the facts that you won't see in the news - at least not yet:

**

I THINK IT IS REMARKABLE THAT WITHIN A WEEK OF TIGER WOODS CRASHING HIS ESCALADE, THE PRESS FOUND EVERY WOMAN WITH WHOM TIGER HAS HAD AN AFFAIR IN THE LAST FEW YEARS, WITH PHO-

TOS, TEXT MESSAGES, RECORDED PHONE CALLS, ETC.

AND, THEY NOT ONLY KNOW THE CAUSE OF THE FAMILY FIGHT, BUT THEY EVEN KNOW IT WAS A WEDGE FROM HIS GOLF BAG THAT HIS WIFE USED TO BREAK OUT THE WINDOWS IN THE ESCALADE.

NOT ONLY THAT, THEY KNOW WHICH WEDGE !!!!!

AND EACH AND EVERY DAY, THEY GIVE AMERICA MORE UPDATES ON HIS SEX-REHAB STAY, HIS WIFE'S PLANS FOR DI-VORCE,   AND THE DATES AND TOURNA-MENTS HE WILL PLAY IN.

OBAMA HAS BEEN IN OFFICE FOR OVER A YEAR NOW, AND THIS SAME PRESS:

- STILL CANNOT FIND ANY OF HIS CHILD-HOOD FRIENDS OR NEIGHBORS

- OR LOCATE ANY OF OBAMA'S COLLEGE PAPERS OR GRADES

Ron Berger 238

- OR HOW HE PAID FOR A HARVARD EDU-
CATION

- OR WHICH COUNTRY ISSUED HIS VISA TO
TRAVEL TO PAKISTAN IN THE 1980'S

- OR BARRY SOTORO'S OR EVEN MICHELLE
OBAMA'S PRINCETON THESIS ON RACISIM.

THEY JUST CAN'T SEEM TO FIND THEM !!!!!

YET THE PUBLIC STILL TRUSTS THAT SAME
PRESS TO GIVE THEM THE WHOLE TRUTH !

TRULY REMARKABLE !!!

****

One of our biggest problems in our country is that we forget too quickly and forgive too quickly. The impact of 9-11 has faded away and we hardly have feelings for that day anymore. How can we forget that over 3,000 of our people died that day and the Muslims celebrated. Can't we come to grips with the magnitude of this atrocity and keep in mind that they who perpetrated this on us continue to plot our demise.

President Bush called it correctly - we are in a "war on terrorism" and we can't forget that. This war is destined to last years. We now have a president that refuses to call a "spade a spade" and doesn't even want his "lackeys" to mention that Islam is an evil movement, bent on KILLING.

Knowledgeable people have repeated time and time again that BO is a Muslim and therefore under their law to "change the world". That change is to socialize the USA - the last great bastion of freedom - and turn it into a State of Islam.

The truth speaks for itself. Below is some of Brigitte Gabriel's speech delivered at the Intelligence Summit in Washington DC. You may need to read it several times to digest it all. She gave this at Duke University also. In today's world, this has to be considered .

**

EVERY AMERICAN NEEDS TO READ THIS!

Editor's Note: Below are selected excerpts from Brigitte Gabriel's speech delivered at the Intelligence Summit in Washington DC

We gather here today to share information and knowledge. Intelligence is not merely cold hard data about numerical strength or armament or disposition of military forces. The most important element of intelligence has to be understanding the mindset and intention of the enemy. The

West has been wallowing in a state of ignorance and denial for thirty years as Muslim extremist perpetrated evil against innocent victims in the name of Allah.

I was ten years old when my home exploded around me, burying me under the rubble and leaving me to drink my blood to survive, as the perpetrators shouted, 'Allah Akbar!' My only crime was that I was a Christian living in a Christian town. At 10 years old, I learned the meaning of the word 'infidel.'

I had a crash course in survival. Not in the Girl Scouts, but in a bomb shelter where I lived for seven years in pitch darkness, freezing cold, drinking stale water and eating grass to live. At the age of 13, dressed in my burial clothes going to bed at night, waiting to be slaughtered. By the age of 20, I had buried most of my friends--killed by Muslims. We were not Americans living in New York , or Britons in London . We were Arab Christians living in Lebanon .

As a victim of Islamic terror, I was amazed when I saw Americans waking up on September 12, 2001, and asking themselves 'Why do they hate us?' The psychoanalyst experts were coming up with all sort of excuses as to what did we do to offend the Muslim World. But if America and the West were paying attention to the Middle East they would not have had to ask the question. Simply put, they hate us because we are defined in their eyes by one simple word: 'infidels.'

Under the banner of Islam 'la, ilaha illa Allah, muhammad rasoulu Allah,' (None is god except Allah; Muhammad is the Messenger of Allah) they murdered Jewish children in Israel, massacred Christians in Lebanon, killed Copts in Egypt, Assyrians in Syria, Hindus in India, and expelled almost 900,000 Jews from Muslim lands. We Middle Eastern infidels paid the price then. Now infidels worldwide are paying the price for indifference and shortsightedness.

Tolerating evil is a crime. Appeasing murderers doesn't buy protection. It earns one disrespect and loathing in the enemy's eyes. Yet apathy is the weapon by which the West is committing suicide. Political correctness forms the shackles around our ankles, by which Islamist's are leading us to our demise.

America and the West are doomed to failure in this war unless they stand up and identify the real enemy: Islam. You hear about Cahaba and Salafi Islam as the only extreme form of Islam. All the other Muslims, supposedly, are wonderful moderates. Closer to the truth are the pictures of the irrational eruption of violence in reaction to the cartoons of Mohammed printed by a Danish newspaper. From burning embassies, to calls to butcher those who mock Islam, to warnings that the West be prepared for another holocaust, those pictures have given us a glimpse into the real face of the enemy. News pictures and video of these events represent a canvas of hate decorated by different nationalities who share one common ideology of hate, bigotry and intolerance derived from one source: authentic Islam. An Islam that is awakening from centuries of slumber to re-ignite its wrath against the infidel and dominate the world. An Islam which has declared 'Intifada' on the West.

America and the West can no longer afford to lay in their lazy state of overweight ignorance. The consequences of this mental disease are starting to attack the body, and if they don't take the necessary steps now to control it, death will be knocking soon. If you want to understand the nature of the enemy we face, visualize a tapestry of snakes. They slither and they hiss, and they would eat each other alive, but they will unite in a hideous mass to achieve their common goal of imposing Islam on the world.

This is the ugly face of the enemy we are fighting. We are fighting a powerful ideology that is capable of altering basic human instincts. An ideology that can turn a mother into a launching pad of death.. A perfect example is a recently elected Hamas official in the Palestinian Territories who raves in heavenly joy about sending her three sons to death and offering the ones who are still alive for the cause. It is an ideology that is capable of offering highly educated individuals such as doctors and lawyers far more joy in attaining death than any respect and stature life in society is ever capable of giving them.

The United States has been a prime target for radical Islamic hatred and terror. Every Friday, mosques in the Middle East ring with shrill prayers and monotonous chants calling death, destruction and damnation down on America and its people. The radical Islamist deeds have been as vile as their words. Since the Iran hostage crisis, more than three thousand Americans have died in a terror campaign almost unprecedented in its calculated cruelty along with thousands of other citizens worldwide. Even the Nazis did not turn their own children into human bombs, and then rejoice at their deaths as well the deaths of their victims. This intentional, indiscriminate and wholesale murder of innocent American citizens is justified and glorified in the name of Islam.

America cannot effectively defend itself in this war unless and until the American people understand the nature of the enemy that we face. Even after 9/11 there are those who say that we must engage our terrorist enemies, that we must address their grievances. Their grievance is our freedom of religion. Their grievance is our freedom of speech. Their grievance is our democratic process where the rule of law comes from the voices of many not that of just one prophet. It is the respect we instill in our children towards all religions. It is the equality we grant each other as human beings sharing a planet and striving to make the world a better place for all humanity. Their grievance is the kindness and respect a man shows a woman, the justice we practice as equals under the law, and the mercy we grant our enemy. Their grievance cannot be answered by an apology for who or what we are.

Our mediocre attitude of not confronting Islamic forces of bigotry and hatred wherever they raised their ugly head in the last 30 years, has empowered and strengthened our enemy to launch a full scale attack on the very freedoms we cherish in their effort to impose their values and way of life on our civilization.

If we don't wake up and challenge our Muslim community to take action against the terrorists within it, if we don't believe in ourselves as Americans and in the standards we should hold every patriotic American to, we are going to pay a price for our delusion. For the sake of our children and our country, we must wake up and take action. In the face of a torrent of hateful invective and terrorist murder, America 's learning curve since the Iran hostage crisis is so shallow that it is almost flat. The longer we lay supine, the more difficult it will be to stand erect.

This is all coming true. A non-patriot is President of this great country. He has openly admitted his Muslim roots and his sympathy for all Muslims. How can this happen?? APATHY, that's how!!! Send this around.

Brigitte Gabriel is an expert on the Middle East conflict and lectures nationally and internationally on the subject. She's the former news anchor of World News for Middle East television and the founder of AmericanCongressforTruth.com

****

While the Congress is dismissing our "war on terrorism" they continually take up the battle on "extremely important issues" such as:

**

Black hurricanes...Well, it appears our African-American friends have found yet something else to be pissed about. A black congress-woman (this would be Sheila Jackson Lee, of Houston), reportedly complained that the names of hurricanes are all Caucasian sounding names.

She would prefer some names that reflect African American culture such as Chamiqua, Tanisha, Woeisha, Shaqueal, and Jamal. I am NOT making this up!

She would also like the weather reports to be broadcast in 'language' that street people can understand because one of the problems that happened in New Orleans was, that black people couldn't understand the seriousness of the

situation, due to the racially biased language of the weather report.

I guess if the weather person says that the winds are going to blow at 140+ MPH, that's to hard to understand.

I can hear it now: A weatherman in New Orleans says...........Wazzup, mutha-fukkas!

Hehr-i-cane Chamiqua be headin' fo' yo ass like Leroy on a crotch rocket! Bitch be a category fo'! So, turn off dem chitlins, grab yo' chirren, leave yo crib, and head fo' de nearest FEMA office fo yo FREE shit.

****

Some of my black friends may take offense to the above, but it's the truth - no matter what you think. And yes - you are not African-American - you are black. Just like I'm white and the Indians are red and the orientals are yellow. Many of you would have trouble pointing to Africa on the map and for sure have no idea how your ancestral lineage goes. I am not a German-American or my wife an English-American, we are AMERICANS and the sooner you come to this realization the better the whole country will be.

I don't give a crap about being "politically correct". The best goal we can aspire to is being a "correct American". This country was founded on diversity, but it was grounded in the Christian/Judaeo religion and all our fore-fathers agreed that it should be well established that no one would have any doubts about our beliefs.

Now we are getting "leaders" that want to change that. Believe me, God has not changed - we have. God is the same yesterday, today and forever.

Why do these people want to change us? Mohammed is not God. It's like worshiping the golden calf. Lot of good that will do you. God has given us the ability to change things back and put Him in the middle of our universe again. How many times do you think God will "suffer" us? I'm sure that He is getting anxious about our desire to serve Him and only Him. We need to take action before it is too late. We only get one life to do the right thing and if we mess it up there are no "do-overs or mulligans".

Many black people were so happy when BO became president. Mainly because he was the first "black" president. And now, he is making a mockery out of the office and bowing to the King of Saudi Arabia, deleting National Prayer Day, being disrespectful to our flag, lying to the voters - saying one thing and doing another, turning our freedoms into socialism, bankrupting our economy, hiring misfits, liars, tax cheats and totally unqualified minions to do the dirty work he is proposing. Plus that - he is NOT qualified for the job as president. First - he has done nothing to give him experience for the job and second - he is not a citizen qualified to be there. He was born in KENYA, AFRICA and not the USA. The law expressly forbids people from this office if they are "foreign born". That's the way it is and why haven't our "illustrious" freedom of the press people brought this up? It's amazing what they can do if they really want to.

**

Transcript – We The People by Nos Populus

Dear President Obama,

"We The People" have stated resolutely we reject your vision for our country. You claim you have not heard us.

"We The People" have assembled across America resisting your efforts to subvert our constitution and undermine our liberty. You claim you have not seen us.

Since you have not acknowledged our

message, let us here present it once more for if as President Wilson said, "a leader's ear must ring with the voices of the people," the time has come.

Our greatest treasure is freedom – the absence of restraints on our ability to think and to act. The corollary of freedom is individual responsibility. We believe in the power of the individual.

A few years ago President Bush said, "History moves toward freedom because the desire for freedom is written in every human heart." Let us add that we will preserve it only as long as devotion to freedom is expressed in the heart of our actions.

When President Lincoln dedicated Gettysburg National Cemetery he declared, "It is for us the living to be dedicated here to the unfinished work which they who fought here have thus so nobly advanced."

That unfinished cause for which our soldiers willingly go to battle and for which so many have given their lives is a free

United States of America. It has been nearly one hundred fifty years and the work President Lincoln spoke of is not finished. In fact, that work will never be finished.

Freedom is the capacity of self-determination. It is not an entity but a condition and conditions change. Freedom can expand, yet so can it contract.

You promised change when you took office, Mr. President, but subjugation is not change we wanted or will accept.

You have expanded government, violated our Constitution, confounded laws, seized private industry, destroyed jobs, perverted our economy, curtailed free speech, corrupted our currency, weakened our national security, and endangered our sovereignty.

By compromising our nation's cultural, legal and economic institutions, you are ensuring that our children will never achieve the same quality of life as we enjoy today. Through generational theft you are robbing the unborn of opportunity.

This is not acceptable. Not in America. We did not become a strong nation through hope but rather through self-reliance.

No one better understands the relationship between individual achievement, dignity and strength than our armed forces. Through every war our soldiers have held this nation's destiny in their hands. They have not failed us. They cherish freedom enough that they are willing to die for it.

Our duty to them and to ourselves is to treasure freedom enough to live up to it.

We accept the challenge, Mr. President. That is why we are assembling across the land to deliver our message to you as often and in every way we can. Dismiss us at your political peril.

Our great nation is a Republic. We will not accept tyranny under any guise. Your policy to redistribute the fruits of our labor is Statism and will not be tolerated.

By our honor, Mr. President, we vow forever to resist coercive government in America. Patriots will not stand silent as you attempt to dismantle the greatest nation on earth. "We The People" will defend our liberty. We will protect our beloved country and America's exceptionalism will prevail.

God Bless the United States of America!

Sincerely,

We The People

****

Things are getting so bad that even other countries are noticing how strange the US has become. Those that were our friends and allies are now on the "not wanted list". The transparency of these disgraceful acts is so apparent that we are dangerously close to being alone in our fight against terrorism. When the "others" see that we have lost the will to fight - they will no longer be able to carry on. The war will be lost and BO and his band of minions will claim victory in the name of Mohammed and tell us that the world is at peace.

I hope that I don't have to remind you that The Bible talks about those that will show their faces as the Messiah and many will be taken in. But, throughout the Bible are warnings that need to be taken seriously.

**

ANTICHRIST

Taken from the HOLY BIBLE: NEW INTERNATIONAL VERSION (C) 1978 by the New

York Bible Society, used by permission of Zondervan Bible Publishers.

MAT 24:5 For many will come in my name, claiming, 'I am the Christ,' and will deceive many.

23 At that time if anyone says to you, 'Look, here is the Christ!' or, 'There he is!' do not believe it.

24 For false Christs and false prophets will appear and perform great

signs and miracles to deceive even the elect--if that were possible.

26 "So if anyone tells you, 'There he is, out in the desert,' do not go out; or, 'Here he is, in the inner rooms,' do not believe it.

MAR 13:6 Many will come in my name, claiming, 'I am he,' and will deceive many.

21 At that time if anyone says to you, 'Look, here is the Christ!' or, 'Look, there he is!' do not believe it.

22 For false Christs and false prophets will appear and perform signs and

miracles to deceive the elect--if that were possible.

LUK 21:8 He replied: "Watch out that you are not deceived. For many will come in my name, claiming, 'I am he,' and, 'The time is near.' Do not follow them.

2TH 2:3 Don't let anyone deceive you in any way, for that day will not come until the rebellion occurs and the man of lawlessness is revealed, the man doomed to destruction.

4   He will oppose and will exalt himself over everything that is called God or is worshiped, so that he sets himself up in God's temple, proclaiming himself to be God.

5   Don't you remember that when I was with you I used to tell you these things?

6 And now you know what is holding him back, so that he may be revealed at

the proper time.

7 For the secret power of lawlessness is already at work; but the one who now holds it back will continue to do so till he is taken out of the way.

8   And then the lawless one will be revealed, whom the Lord Jesus will overthrow with the breath of his mouth and destroy by the splendor of his coming.

9 The coming of the lawless one will be in accordance with the work of Satan displayed in all kinds of counterfeit miracles, signs and wonders,

10 and in every sort of evil that deceives those who are perishing. They perish because they refused to love the truth and so be saved.

11   For this reason God sends them a powerful delusion so that they will

believe the lie

12   and so that all will be condemned who have not believed the truth but have delighted in wickedness.

1JO 2:18   Dear children, this is the last hour; and as you have heard that the antichrist is coming, even now many antichrists have come. This is how we know it is the last hour.

22   Who is the liar? It is the man who denies that Jesus is the Christ. Such a man is the antichrist--he denies the Father and the Son.

4:3   but every spirit that does not acknowledge Jesus is not from God. This is the spirit of the antichrist, which you have heard is coming and even now is already in the world.

2JO 1:7   Many deceivers, who do not acknowledge Jesus Christ as coming in the flesh, have gone out into the world. Any such person is the deceiver and the antichrist.

REV 19:20   But the beast was captured, and with him the false prophet who had performed the miraculous signs on his behalf. With these signs he had deluded those who had received the mark of the beast and worshiped his image. The two of them were thrown alive into the fiery lake of burning sulfur.

20:10 And the devil, who deceived them, was thrown into the lake of burning sulfur, where the beast and the false prophet had been thrown. They will be tormented day and night for ever and ever.

15 If anyone's name was not found written in the book of life, he was thrown into the lake of fire.

Bible Bulletin Board

internet: www.biblebb.com

modem: 609-324-9187

Box 318

Columbus, NJ 08022

....online since 1986

Sysop/Webmaster: Tony Capoccia

ROM 16:17 I urge you, brothers, to watch out for those who cause divisions and put obstacles in your way that are contrary to the teaching you have learned. Keep away from them.

18   For such people are not serving our Lord Christ, but their own appetites. By smooth talk and flattery they deceive the minds of naive people.

****

Naive people are deceived.   If a person isn't qualified to be president, he should be run out of town on a rail. Here is proof that BO is NOT QUALIFIED to be president:

**

If this be true, then let's do something crazy, try honoring the law and taking this man out of office and prosecute him for fraud and perjury and every other law he has violated willfully. After all, it's the law, stupid".   Amazing how many lawyers are so ignorant to the law.

Ron Berger 262

Now let's see what the US politicians and judges will now do about this non-qualifying president.

The American people have been fooled.

This is part of what Obama has spent almost $2M to hide.

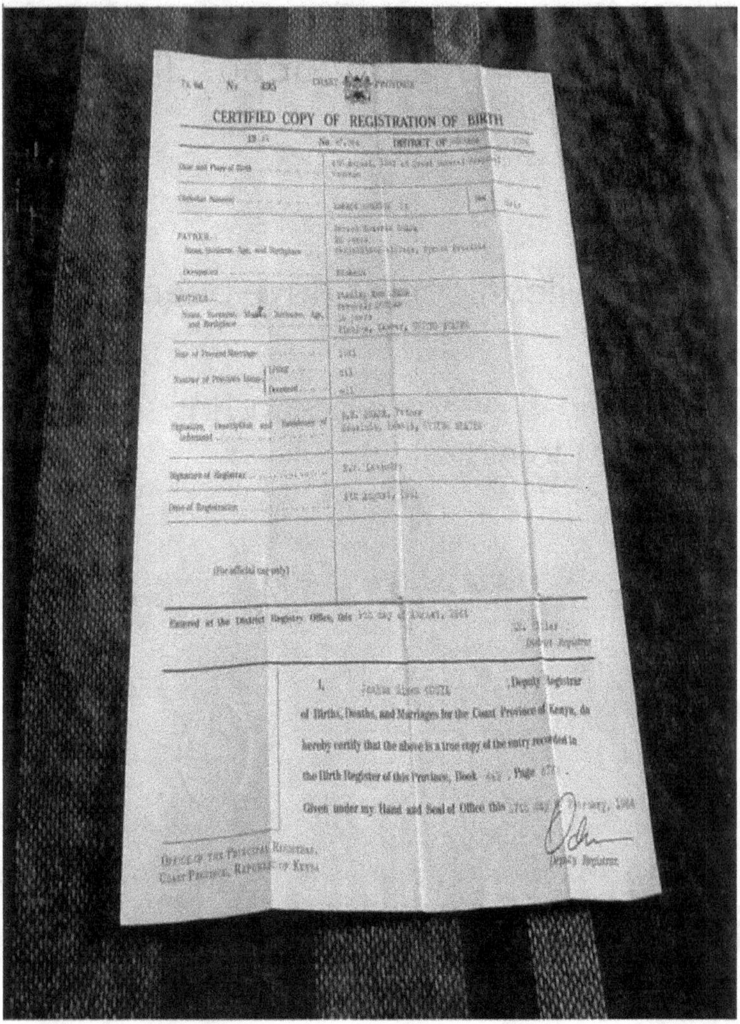

CERTIFIED COPY OF REGISTRATION OF BIRTH

Date and Place of Birth

Christian Name(s)

FATHER

Occupation

MOTHER

Signature of Registrar

Date of Registration

(For official use only)

Entered at the District Registry Office, this

Deputy Registrar

I, , Deputy Registrar of Births, Deaths, and Marriages for the Coast Province of Kenya, do hereby certify that the above is a true copy of the entry recorded in the Birth Register of this Province, Book , Page .

Given under my Hand and Seal of Office this

Deputy Registrar

Office of the Principal Registrar, Coast Province, Republic of Kenya

CERTIFIED COPY OF REGISTRATION OF BIRTH

Certificate of registration of birth for Barack Hussein Obama II, showing date and place of birth 4th August, 1961 at Coast General Hospital, Mombasa; father Barack Hussein Obama, 25 years, of Kanyadhiang village, Nyanza Province, occupation Student; mother Stanley Ann Obama, formerly Dunham, 18 years, of Wichita, Kansas, United States; signed by registrar E.F. Lavender, dated 5th August, 1961.

I asked a British history buff I know if he could find out who the colonial registrar was for Mombasa in 1961.

He called me up a few minutes ago and said "Sir Edward F. Lavender"

Source(s): "Kenya Dominion Record 4667 Australian library."

Posted by Alan Peters at 11:56 PM

Testimony from a Mombasa science teacher and the Mombasa Registrar of births that Obama's birth certificate from Mombasa is genuine. A copy of President Obama's birth certificate that Lucas Smith obtained through the help of a Kenyan Colonel who got it recently directly from the Coast General Hospital in Mombasa , Kenya .

COAST PROVINCE GENERAL HOSPITAL

Mombasa. British Protectorate of Kenya.

CERTIFICATE OF BIRTH

Certificate No. 32018

Child bearing the name **BARACK HUSSEIN OBAMA II** / Sex **M**

was born to

STANLEY ANN OBAMA	DUNHAM	11/29/1942
Full Name of Mother	Maiden Surname	Date of Birth

BARACK HUSSEIN OBAMA		1936
Full Name of Father		Date of Birth

on this **4th day of AUGUST, 1961** at **7:24 PM**

7 pounds 1 ounce	18 inches	6 inches
Weight of Child at Birth	Length	Width Between Shoulders

HONOLULU, HAWAII, UNITED STATES	WICHITA, KANSAS, UNITED STATES
Residence of Mother	Birth Place of Mother

KANYADHIANG VILLAGE, NYANZA	STUDENT	STUDENT
Birth Place of Father	Occupation of Father	Occupation of Mother

JAMES O. W. ANG'AWA		8/8/1961
Name of Attending Doctor	Signature of Attending Doctor	Date

JOHN KWAME ODONGO

Supervisor of Obstetrics

8-7-1961

Signature · Date

V452
M37

Global Elite Picked Obama Long Before Voters

Man recounts startling tale of first time he heard of Barack Obama—18 years ago in Russia

By Tom Fife

During the period of roughly February 1992 to mid-1994, I was making frequent trips to Moscow in the process of starting a software development, joint-venture company with some people from the Russian scientific community. One of the men in charge on the Russian side was named V. M.; he had a wife named T.M. V. was a level-headed scientist, while his wife was rather deeply committed to the losing communist cause.

Early in 1992, the American half of our venture was invited to V. & T.'s Moscow flat as we were about to return to the States. As the evening wore on, T. developed a decidedly rough anti-American edge—one her husband tried to quietly rein in.

The bottom line of the tirade she started against the United States went something like this: "You Americans always like to think that you have the perfect government and your people are always so perfect. Well then, why haven't you had a woman president by now?"

You had a chance to vote for a woman vice president and you didn't do it."

The general response went along the lines that you don't vote for someone just because of their sex. Besides, you don't vote for vice president, but the president and vice president as a ticket.

"Well, I think you are going to be surprised when you get a black president very soon," she said. The consensus we expressed was that we didn't think there was anything innately barring that. The right time and sure, America would try to vote for the right person, be he or she, black or not.

"What if I told you that you will have a black president very soon and he will be a communist?" she said. "Well, you will; and he will be a communist."

One of us asked, "It sounds like you know something we don't know."

"Yes, it is true," she replied. "This is not some idle talk. He is already born, and he is educated and being groomed to be president right now. You will be impressed to know that he has gone to the best schools

of presidents. He is what you call 'Ivy League.' You don't believe me, but he is real and I even know his name. His name is Barack. His mother is white and American and his father is black from Africa. That's right, a chocolate baby! And he's going to be president."

She became more and more smug as she presented her stream of detailed knowledge and predictions so matter-of-factly—as though all were foregone conclusions. "It's all been thought out. His father is not an American black, so he won't have that social slave stigma. He is intelligent and he is half white and has been raised from the cradle to be an atheist and a communist. He's gone to the finest schools. He is being guided every step of the way and he will be irresistible to America."

She was obviously happy that the communists were doing this and that it would somehow be a thumbing of their collective noses at America: They would give us a black president and he'd be a communist to boot. She made it obvious that she thought that this was going to breathe new life into world communism. She always asserted that communism was far from dead.

She was full of details about him that she was eager to relate. She rattled off a complete litany. He was from Hawaii. He went to school in California. He lived in Chicago. He was soon to be elected to the legislature. "Have no doubt: he is one of us, a Soviet."

Since I had dabbled in languages, I knew a smattering of Arabic. I commented: "If I remember correctly, 'Barack' comes from the Arabic word for 'blessing.' That seems to be an odd name for an American." She replied quickly, "Yes. It is 'African,'" she insisted, "and he will be a blessing for world communism. We will regain our strength and become the No. 1 power in the world."

She said something to the effect that America was at the same time the great hope and the great obstacle for communism. America would have to be converted to communism, and Barack was going to pave the way.

Well, it's definitely anecdotal. It doesn't prove that Obama has had Soviet communist training nor that he was groomed to be the first black American president, but it does show one thing that I think is important. It shows that Soviet Russian communists knew of Barack from a very early date. It also shows that they truly believed among themselves that he was raised and groomed communist to pave the way for their future. This report on Barack came personally to me from one of them long before America knew he existed.

Although I had never before heard of him, at the time of this conversation Obama was 30-plus years old and was obviously touted enough that he was their anticipated rising star.

★

Who is Tom Fife?

Tom Fife was a government contractor with an active security clearance who took notes on his trips for Defense Intelligence Agency debriefings within the Department of Defense. In 1992, following an astounding conversation at a dinner party in Moscow, he took down notes for future reference. It was long before the world ever heard the name "Barack Obama."

Students of revisionist history will remember that Bill Clinton disappeared from Oxford University in England for a while in 1970 and surfaced in Moscow (courtesy of the CIA) purportedly to be trained in communism. When the accompanying story first appeared, we could not locate its source for confirmation and cast it off as a probable Internet fairy tale. But we have since interviewed Tom Fife, blended the information with the many accusations of high-profile politicos (such as former UN Ambassador Alan Keyes) and witnessed the communistic behavior of the White House occupant, and we have no doubt as to the authenticity of this amazing piece. —Ed.

The above article is hard to read. Sorry I can't make it any larger but, it would be worth your time to get a magnifying glass and read it.

Tom Fife in the American Free Press was in Moscow in 1992 where a member of the Russian Academy of Sciences stated they had trained a Barack Obama as a communist and atheist and he will make easier the triumph of communism over the USA. The article is at the bottom of this home page regarding the birth of Barack Hussein Obama II in Mombasa , Kenya. Grandmother of President Barack Hussein Obama, Jr. reveals below the story of his birth in Mombasa, Kenya , a seaport, after his mother suffered labor pains while swimming at ocean beach in Mombasa.

"On August 4, 1961 Obama's mother, father and grandmother were attending a Muslim festival in Mombassa , Kenya . Mother had been refused entry to airplanes due to her 9 month pregnancy. It was a hot August day at the festival so the Obama's went to the beach to cool off. While swimming in the ocean, his mother experienced labor pains so was rushed to the Coast Provincial General Hospital, Mombasa, Kenya where Obama was born a few hours later at 7:21pm on August 4, 1961. Four days later his mother flew to Hawaii and registered his birth in Honolulu as a certificate of live birth which omitted the place and hospital of birth."

The local Imam in Mombasa named Barack with his middle name Hussein so his official name on his certificate of live birth below is Barack Hussein Obama, II.

President Obama's Certificate of Live Birth, FORGED by one of his workers named John.

Barack Hussein Obama is the first U.S. president born in Africa at the Coast Provincial General Hospital, Mombasa, K - enya. The Hawaii Certificate of Live Birth below is a forgery and of no value.

CERTIFICATION OF LIVE BIRTH

STATE OF HAWAII
HONOLULU

DEPARTMENT OF HEALTH
HAWAII U.S.A.

CERTIFICATE NO.

CHILD'S NAME
BARACK HUSSEIN OBAMA II

DATE OF BIRTH
August 4, 1961

HOUR OF BIRTH
7:24 PM

SEX
MALE

CITY, TOWN OR LOCATION OF BIRTH
HONOLULU

ISLAND OF BIRTH
OAHU

COUNTY OF BIRTH
HONOLULU

MOTHER'S MAIDEN NAME
STANLEY ANN DUNHAM

MOTHER'S RACE
CAUCASIAN

FATHER'S NAME
BARACK HUSSEIN OBAMA

FATHER'S RACE
AFRICAN

DATE FILED BY REGISTRAR
August 8, 1961

This copy serves as prima facie evidence of the fact of birth in any court proceeding. [HRS 338-13(b), 338-19]

ANY ALTERATIONS INVALIDATE THIS CERTIFICATE

While you were watching the oil spill, the New York failed terrorist bombing and other critical crises, Hillary Clinton signed the small arms treaty with the UN.

OBAMA FINDS LEGAL WAY AROUND THE 2ND AMENDMENT AND USES IT IF THIS PASSES, THERE COULD BE WAR

On Wednesday Obama

Took the First Major Step in a Plan to Ban All Firearms in the United States. The Obama administration intends to force gun control and a complete ban on all weapons for US citizens through the signing of international treaties with foreign nations. By signing international treaties on gun control, the Obama administration can use the US State Department to bypass the normal legislative process in Congress. Once the US Government signs these international treaties, all US citizens will be subject to those gun laws created by foreign governments. These are laws that have been developed and promoted by organizations such as the

United Nations and individuals such as George Soros and Michael Bloomberg. The laws are designed and intended to lead to the complete ban and confiscation of all firearms. The Obama administration is attempting to use tactics and methods of gun control that will inflict major damage to our 2nd Amendment before US citizens even understand what has happened.

Obama can appear before the public and tell them that he does not intend to pursue any legislation (in the United States) that will lead to new gun control laws, while cloaked in secrecy, his Secretary of State, Hillary Clinton is committing the US to international treaties and foreign gun control laws. Does that mean Obama is telling the truth? What it means is that there will be no publicized gun control debates in the media or votes in Congress. We will wake up one morning and find that the United States has signed a treaty that prohibits firearm and ammunition manufacturers from selling to the public. We will wake up another morning and find that the US has signed a treaty that prohibits any transfer of firearm ownership. And then, we will wake up yet another morning and find that the US has signed a treaty that requires US citizens to deliver any firearm they own to the local government collection and destruction center or face imprisonment. This has happened in other countries, past and present! THIS IS NOT A JOKE OR A FALSE WARNING.

As sure as government health care will be forced on us by the Obama administration through whatever means necessary, so will gun control..

Read the Article U.S. reverses stance on treaty to regulate arms trade

WASHINGTON (Reuters) - The United States reversed policy on Wednesday and said it would back launching talks on a treaty to regulate arms sales as long as the talks operated by consensus, a stance critics said gave every nation a veto. The decision, announced in a statement released by the U.S. State Department, overturns the position of former President George W. Bush's administration, which had opposed such a treaty on the grounds that national controls were better.

This is a very serious matter! Silence will lead us to Socialism!!!

WRITTEN BY A 15 yr. Old SCHOOL KID IN ARIZONA:

New Pledge of Allegiance ?(TOTALLY AWESOME)!

Since the Pledge of Allegiance and The Lord's Prayer Are not allowed in most Public schools anymore because the word 'God' is mentioned.....
A kid in Arizona wrote this poem

NEW School prayer:

Now I sit me down in school
Where praying is against the rule
For this great nation under God
Finds mention of Him very odd.

If scripture now the class recites,
It violates the Bill of Rights.
And anytime my head I bow
Becomes a Federal matter now.

Ron Berger 274

Our hair can be purple, orange or green,
That's no offense; it's a freedom scene..
The law is specific, the law is precise.
Prayers spoken aloud are a serious vice.

For praying in a public hall
Might offend someone with no faith at all..
In silence alone we must meditate,
God's name is prohibited by the state.

We're allowed to cuss and dress like freaks,
And pierce our noses, tongues and cheeks...
They've outlawed guns, but FIRST the Bible.
To quote the Good Book makes me liable.

We can elect a pregnant Senior Queen,
And the 'unwed daddy,' our Senior King.
It's 'inappropriate' to teach right from wrong,

Ron Berger 275

We're taught that such 'judgments' do not belong...

We can get our condoms and birth controls,
Study witchcraft, vampires and totem poles..
But the Ten Commandments are not allowed,
No word of God must reach this crowd.

It's scary here I must confess,

When chaos reigns the school's a mess.

So, Lord, this silent plea I make:

Should I be shot; My soul please take!

Amen

****

More Surprises

I was about to wind this book up and then realized that there were several other items that just needed to be brought up:

**

This was written by a man in his mid 80,s very bright and very active was recently awarded France's highest military honor..,actually stormed the beaches in Normandy-quite a man.

The Obama Administration is crowing that they have created 431,000 NEW jobs. What a joke! 411,000 of them are for the Census. How long is that going to last? And, where do they go when the census is finished?

Remember, folks, it was much more important to take over health care, the banks, the auto industry and student loans.   Oh yes, don't forget cap and trade. The stock market is down over 300 points today. Where do we go from here, Mr. President?

Quote: "We will have an open and transparent government. There will be full and open debate on TV so that everyone can see Congress in operation.   We will not do the people's business in secrecy. We will change the way business is done in Washington."   Barack said all those things and you believed him.   And you LIBERALS voted for him.   A YEAR AGO I TOLD YOU IN MY PUBLISHED   'LETTER TO THE EDITOR' THIS WOULD NOT HAPPEN. I TOLD YOU NOT TO BE MESMERIZED BY AN ELOQUENT TALKER BUT YOU WERE TAKEN IN and the whole country is suffering the consequences.

Chicago-style politics continues to rule the day.   There was the alleged payoff for Obama's Senate seat. Then they tried to buy off Joe Sestak in PA. What's the latest in Colorado with Andrew Romanoff?   Jobs seem to be available for politicians on a grand scale. How about the people? When is there going to be a concerted effort to encourage job creation amongst the private sector?

Did you see, too, Hillary Clinton, Secretary of State, signing onto a United Nations Resolution to ban the ownership of guns by private citizens? This is the administration's ploy to take away our guns and go around the 2nd amendment to the U.S. Constitution. This administration does not read nor does it try to follow the Constitution as it was written. Where in the Constitution does it give the federal government the right to take over health care or education? Please, someone show me. These are the responsibilities of the States.

What is truly unfortunate, however, is that it is not over. Obama already has the FCC working on new rules for free speech and the air waves. Since he's having difficulty with 'the Fairness Doctrine" he wants them to come up with ways to shut down conservative radio talk show hosts and, of course, FOX News. One of the ideas they are working on is a new definition for hate speech. They would like to bar any 'criticism of the administration' and if they can call it hate speech they can shut you down. Isn't this what Chavez did in Venezuela? And we must not forget Mao in China and Stalin in the USSR. This is what Socialists do and this administration continues to move in that direction.

November cannot come too soon!!!! I hope that you will remember when you go into the voting booth how this administration is taking away your freedom.

****

The following lists are very revealing. Please see if your Representative or elected official is among the group:

**

How Many Members Of The U.S. Congress Are Self-Declared Socialists?

Updated for the 111th Congress

The following FAQ will help clarify a few facts:

Q: What is the Socialist International?

A: It is the worldwide organization of socialist, social democratic and labor parties. It currently brings together 131 political parties and organizations from all continents. Its origins go back to the early international organizations of the labor movement of the last century.* It has existed in its present form since 1951, when it was re-established at the Frankfurt Congress. They are now headquartered in London, England.

* In 1864, representatives of English and French industrial workers founded the International Workingmen's Association in London. Karl Marx, who was living in London at the time, became the First International's dominant figure. Marx's doctrines were revived in the 20th century by Russian revolutionary Vladimir Ilich Lenin, who developed and applied them – and we all know that what was started as a labor movement ended up as the biggest totalitarian/communist state, i.e., the USSR.

Q: What is the Democratic Socialists of America [DSA]?

A: It is the largest socialist organization in the United States, and the principal U.S. affiliate of the Socialist International. Their website is http://www.dsausa.org/dsa.html

Q: What are seven principles behind what the DSA's calls it's "Progressive Challenge?"

Dignified Work

Environmental Justice

Economic Redistribution

Democratic Participation

Community Empowerment

Global Non-Violence

Social Justice.

Never mind their soothing-sounding leftist doublespeak like 'Environmental Justice' (whatever that is supposed to mean) or the soft & fuzzy 'Global Non-Violence' (a euphemism for unilateral disarmament) - the DSA's self-declared principle of 'Economic Redistribution' clearly shows where these folks are coming from and exactly where they plan to take America.

Q: How many members of the U.S. Congress are also members of the DSA?

A: Seventy!

Q: How many of the DSA members sit on the Judiciary Committee?

A: Eleven: John Conyers [Chairman of the Judiciary Committee], Tammy Baldwin, Jerrold Nadler, Luis Gutierrez, Melvin Watt, Maxine Waters, Hank Johnson, Steve Cohen, Barbara Lee, Robert Wexler, Linda Sanchez [there are 23 Democrats on the Judiciary Committee of which eleven, almost half, are now members of the DSA].

Q: Who are these members of Congress?

A: See the listing below

Co-Chairs

Hon. Raúl M. Grijalva (AZ-07)

Hon. Lynn Woolsey (CA-06)

Vice Chairs

Hon. Diane Watson (CA-33)

Hon. Sheila Jackson-Lee (TX-18)

Hon. Mazie Hirono (HI-02)

Hon. Dennis Kucinich (OH-10)

Senate Members

Hon. Bernie Sanders (VT)

House Members

Hon. Neil Abercrombie (HI-01)

Hon. Tammy Baldwin (WI-02)

Hon. Xavier Becerra (CA-31)

Hon. Madeleine Bordallo (GU-AL)

Hon. Robert Brady (PA-01)

Hon. Corrine Brown (FL-03)

Hon. Michael Capuano (MA-08)

Hon. André Carson (IN-07)

Hon. Donna Christensen (VI-AL)

Hon. Yvette Clarke (NY-11)

Hon. William "Lacy" Clay (MO-01)

Hon. Emanuel Cleaver (MO-05)

Hon. Steve Cohen (TN-09)

Hon. John Conyers (MI-14)

Hon. Elijah Cummings (MD-07)

Hon. Danny Davis (IL-07)

Hon. Peter DeFazio (OR-04)

Hon. Rosa DeLauro (CT-03)

Rep. Donna F. Edwards (MD-04)

Hon. Keith Ellison (MN-05)

Hon. Sam Farr (CA-17)

Hon. Chaka Fattah (PA-02)

Hon. Bob Filner (CA-51)

Hon. Barney Frank (MA-04)

Hon. Marcia L. Fudge (OH-11)

Hon. Alan Grayson (FL-08)

Hon. Luis Gutierrez (IL-04)

Hon. John Hall (NY-19)

Hon. Phil Hare (IL-17)

Hon. Maurice Hinchey (NY-22)

Hon. Michael Honda (CA-15)

Hon. Jesse Jackson, Jr. (IL-02)

Hon. Eddie Bernice Johnson (TX-30)

Hon. Hank Johnson (GA-04)

Hon. Marcy Kaptur (OH-09)

Hon. Carolyn Kilpatrick (MI-13)

Hon. Barbara Lee (CA-09)

Hon. John Lewis (GA-05)

Hon. David Loebsack (IA-02)

Hon. Ben R. Lujan (NM-3)

Hon. Carolyn Maloney (NY-14)

Hon. Ed Markey (MA-07)

Hon. Jim McDermott (WA-07)

Hon. James McGovern (MA-03)

Hon. George Miller (CA-07)

Hon. Gwen Moore (WI-04)

Hon. Jerrold Nadler (NY-08)

Hon. Eleanor Holmes-Norton (DC-AL)

Hon. John Olver (MA-01)

Hon. Ed Pastor (AZ-04)

Hon. Donald Payne (NJ-10)

Hon. Chellie Pingree (ME-01)

Hon. Charles Rangel (NY-15)

Hon. Laura Richardson (CA-37)

Hon. Lucille Roybal-Allard (CA-34)

Hon. Bobby Rush (IL-01)

Hon. Linda Sánchez (CA-47)

Hon. Jan Schakowsky (IL-09)

Hon. José Serrano (NY-16)

Hon. Louise Slaughter (NY-28)

Hon. Pete Stark (CA-13)

Hon. Bennie Thompson (MS-02)

Hon. John Tierney (MA-06)

Hon. Nydia Velazquez (NY-12)

Hon. Maxine Waters (CA-35)

Hon. Mel Watt (NC-12)

Hon. Henry Waxman (CA-30)

Hon. Peter Welch (VT-AL)

Hon. Robert Wexler (FL-19)

Source: Congressional Progressive Caucus

"Victory at all cost. Victory in spite of all terror. Victory no matter how long and how hard the road may be; for without victory there is no survival"
Winston Churchill
May 13, 1940

****

**

Washington, DC

Judicial Watch, the public interest group that investigates and prosecutes government corruption, today released its 2009 list of Washington's "Ten Most Wanted Corrupt Politicians." The list, in alphabetical order, includes:

<u>Senator Christopher Dodd (D-CT)</u>: This marks two years in a row for Senator Dodd, who made the 2008 "Ten Most Corrupt" list for his corrupt relationship with

Fannie Mae and Freddie Mac and for accepting preferential treatment and loan terms from Countrywide Financial, a scandal which still dogs him. In 2009, the scandals kept coming for the Connecticut Democrat. In 2009, Judicial Watch filed a Senate ethics complaint against Dodd for undervaluing a property he owns in Ireland on his Senate Financial Disclosure forms. Judicial Watch's complaint forced Dodd to amend the forms. However, press reports suggest the property to this day remains undervalued. Judicial Watch also alleges in the complaint that Dodd obtained a sweetheart deal for the property in exchange for his assistance in obtaining a presidential pardon (during the Clinton administration) and other favors for a long-time friend and business associate. The false financial disclosure forms were part of the cover-up. Dodd remains the head the Senate Banking Committee.

<u>Senator John Ensign (R-NV)</u>: A number of scandals popped up in 2009 involving public officials who conducted illicit affairs, and then attempted to cover them up with hush payments and favors, an obvious abuse of power. The year's worst

offender might just be Nevada Republican Senator John Ensign. Ensign admitted in June to an extramarital affair with the wife of one of his staff members, who then allegedly obtained special favors from the Nevada Republican in exchange for his silence. According to The New York Times: "The Justice Department and the Senate Ethics Committee are expected to conduct preliminary inquiries into whether Senator John Ensign violated federal law or ethics rules as part of an effort to conceal an affair with the wife of an aide..." The former staffer, Douglas Hampton, began to lobby Mr. Ensign's office immediately upon leaving his congressional job, despite the fact that he was subject to a one-year lobbying ban. Ensign seems to have ignored the law and allowed Hampton lobbying access to his office as a payment for his silence about the affair. (These are potentially criminal offenses.) It looks as if Ensign misused his public office (and taxpayer resources) to cover up his sexual shenanigans.

Rep. Barney Frank (D-MA): Judicial Watch is investigating a $12 million TARP cash injection provided to the Boston-based

OneUnited Bank at the urging of Massachusetts Rep. Barney Frank. As reported in the January 22, 2009, edition of the Wall Street Journal, the Treasury Department indicated it would only provide funds to healthy banks to jump-start lending. Not only was OneUnited Bank in massive financial turmoil, but it was also "under attack from its regulators for allegations of poor lending practices and executive-pay abuses, including owning a Porsche for its executives' use." Rep. Frank admitted he spoke to a "federal regulator," and Treasury granted the funds. (The bank continues to flounder despite Frank's intervention for federal dollars.) Moreover, Judicial Watch uncovered documents in 2009 that showed that members of Congress for years were aware that Fannie Mae and Freddie Mac were playing fast and loose with accounting issues, risk assessment issues and executive compensation issues, even as liberals led by Rep. Frank continued to block attempts to rein in the two Government Sponsored Enterprises (GSEs). For example, during a hearing on September 10, 2003, before the House Committee on Financial Services considering a Bush administration proposal to further regulate Fannie and Freddie, Rep. Frank stated: "I want to begin by saying that I am glad to consider the legislation, but I do not think we are facing any kind of a crisis. That is, in my view, the two Government Sponsored Enterprises we are talking about here, Fannie Mae and Freddie Mac, are not in a crisis. We have recently had an accounting problem with Freddie Mac that has led to people being dismissed, as appears to be appropriate. I do not think at this point there is a problem with a threat to the Treasury." Frank received $42,350 in campaign contributions from Fannie Mae and Freddie Mac between 1989 and 2008. Frank also engaged in a relationship with a Fannie Mae Executive while serving on the House Banking Committee, which has jurisdiction over Fannie Mae and Freddie Mac.

Secretary of Treasury Timothy Geithner: In 2009, Obama Treasury Secretary Timothy Geithner admitted that he failed to pay $34,000 in Social Security and Medicare taxes from 2001-2004 on his lucrative salary at the International Monetary Fund (IMF), an organization with 185 member countries that oversees the global financial system. (Did we mention Geithner now runs the IRS?) It wasn't until President Obama tapped Geithner to head the Treasury Department that he paid back most of the money, although the IRS kindly waived the hefty penalties. In March 2009, Geithner also came under fire for his handling of the AIG bonus scandal, where the company used $165 million of its bailout funds to pay out executive bonuses, resulting in a massive public backlash. Of course as head of the New York Federal Reserve, Geithner helped craft the AIG deal in September 2008. However, when the AIG scandal broke, Geithner claimed he knew nothing of the bonuses until March 10, 2009. The timing is important. According to CNN: "Although Treasury Secretary Timothy Geithner told congressional leaders on Tuesday that he learned of AIG's impending $160 million bonus payments to members of its troubled financial-products unit on March 10, sources tell TIME that the New York Federal Reserve informed Treasury staff that the payments were imminent on Feb. 28. That is ten days before Treasury staffers say they first learned 'full details' of the bonus plan, and three days before the [Obama]

Administration launched a new $30 billion infusion of cash for AIG." Throw in another embarrassing disclosure in 2009 that Geithner employed "household help" ineligible to work in the United States, and it becomes clear why the Treasury Secretary has earned a spot on the "Ten Most Corrupt Politicians in Washington" list.

Attorney General Eric Holder: Tim Geithner can be sure he won't be hounded about his tax-dodging by his colleague Eric Holder, US Attorney General. Judicial Watch strongly opposed Holder because of his terrible ethics record, which includes: obstructing an FBI investigation of the theft of nuclear secrets from Los Alamos Nuclear Laboratory; rejecting multiple requests for an independent counsel to investigate alleged fundraising abuses by then-Vice President Al Gore in the Clinton White House; undermining the criminal investigation of President Clinton by Kenneth Starr in the midst of the Lewinsky investigation; and planning the violent raid to seize then-six-year-old Elian Gonzalez at gunpoint in order to return him to Castro's Cuba. Moreover, there is his soft record on terrorism. Holder bypassed Justice Department procedures to push through Bill Clinton's scandalous presidential pardons and commutations, including for 16 members of FALN, a violent Puerto Rican terrorist group that orchestrated approximately 120 bombings in the United States, killing at least six people and permanently maiming dozens of others, including law enforcement officers. His record in the current administration is no better. As he did during the Clinton administration, Holder continues to ignore serious incidents of corruption that could impact his political bosses at the White House. For example, Holder has refused to investigate charges that the Obama political machine traded VIP access to the White House in exchange for campaign contributions – a scheme eerily similar to one hatched by Holder's former boss, Bill Clinton in the 1990s. The Holder Justice Department also came under fire for dropping a voter intimidation case against the New Black Panther Party. On Election Day 2008, Black Panthers dressed in paramilitary garb threatened voters as they approached polling stations. Holder has also failed to initiate a comprehensive Justice investigation of the notorious organization

ACORN (Association of Community Organizations for Reform Now), which is closely tied to President Obama. There were allegedly more than 400,000 fraudulent ACORN voter registrations in the 2008 campaign. And then there were the journalist videos catching ACORN Housing workers advising undercover reporters on how to evade tax, immigration, and child prostitution laws. Holder's controversial decisions on new rights for terrorists and his attacks on previous efforts to combat terrorism remind many of the fact that his former law firm has provided and continues to provide pro bono representation to terrorists at Guantanamo Bay. Holder's politicization of the Justice Department makes one long for the days of Alberto Gonzales.

Rep. Jesse Jackson, Jr. (D-IL)/ Senator Roland Burris (D-IL): One of the most serious scandals of 2009 involved a scheme by former Illinois Governor Rod Blagojevich to sell President Obama's then-vacant Senate seat to the highest bidder. Two men caught smack dab in the middle of the scandal: Senator Roland Burris, who ultimately got the job, and Rep. Jesse

Jackson, Jr. According to the Chicago Sun-Times, emissaries for Jesse Jackson Jr., named "Senate Candidate A" in the Blagojevich indictment, reportedly offered $1.5 million to Blagojevich during a fundraiser if he named Jackson Jr. to Obama's seat. Three days later federal authorities arrested Blagojevich. Burris, for his part, apparently lied about his contacts with Blagojevich, who was arrested in December 2008 for trying to sell Obama's Senate seat. According to Reuters: "Roland Burris came under fresh scrutiny...after disclosing he tried to raise money for the disgraced former Illinois governor who named him to the U.S. Senate seat once held by President Barack Obama...In the latest of those admissions, Burris said he looked into mounting a fundraiser for Rod Blagojevich -- later charged with trying to sell Obama's Senate seat -- at the same time he was expressing interest to the then-governor's aides about his desire to be appointed." Burris changed his story five times regarding his contacts with Blagojevich prior to the Illinois governor appointing him to the U.S. Senate. Three of those changing explanations came under oath.

<u>President Barack Obama</u>: During his presidential campaign, President Obama promised to run an ethical and transparent administration. However, in his first year in office, the President has delivered corruption and secrecy, bringing Chicago-style political corruption to the White House. Consider just a few Obama administration "lowlights" from year one: Even before President Obama was sworn into office, he was interviewed by the FBI for a criminal investigation of former Illinois Governor Rod Blagojevich's scheme to sell the President's former Senate seat to the highest bidder. (Obama's Chief of Staff Rahm Emanuel and slumlord Valerie Jarrett, both from Chicago, are also tangled up in the Blagojevich scandal.) Moreover, the Obama administration made the startling claim that the Privacy Act does not apply to the White House. The Obama White House believes it can violate the privacy rights of American citizens without any legal consequences or accountability. President Obama boldly proclaimed that "transparency and the rule of law will be the touchstones of this presidency," but his administration is addicted to secrecy,

stonewalling far too many of Judicial Watch's Freedom of Information Act requests and is refusing to make public White House visitor logs as federal law requires. The Obama administration turned the National Endowment of the Arts (as well as the agency that runs the Ameri-Corps program) into propaganda machines, using tax dollars to persuade "artists" to promote the Obama agenda. According to documents uncovered by Judicial Watch, the idea emerged as a direct result of the Obama campaign and enjoyed White House approval and participation. President Obama has installed a record number of "czars" in positions of power. Too many of these individuals are leftist radicals who answer to no one but the president. And too many of the czars are not subject to Senate confirmation (which raises serious constitutional questions). Under the President's bailout schemes, the federal government continues to appropriate or control — through fiat and threats — large sectors of the private economy, prompting conservative columnist George Will to write: "The administration's central activity — the political allocation of wealth and opportunity

— is not merely susceptible to corruption, it is corruption." Government-run health-care and car companies, White House coercion, un-investigated ACORN corruption, debasing his office to help Chicago cronies, attacks on conservative media and the private sector, unprecedented and dangerous new rights for terrorists, perks for campaign donors — this is Obama's "ethics" record — and we haven't even gotten through the first year of his presidency.

<u>Rep. Nancy Pelosi (D-CA)</u>: At the heart of the corruption problem in Washington is a sense of entitlement. Politicians believe laws and rules (even the U.S. Constitution) apply to the rest of us but not to them. Case in point: House Speaker Nancy Pelosi and her excessive and boorish demands for military travel. Judicial Watch obtained documents from the Pentagon in 2009 that suggest Pelosi has been treating the Air Force like her own personal airline. These documents, obtained through the Freedom of Information Act, include internal Pentagon email correspondence detailing attempts by Pentagon staff to accommodate Pelosi's numerous requests

for military escorts and military aircraft as well as the speaker's 11th hour cancellations and changes. House Speaker Nancy Pelosi also came under fire in April 2009, when she claimed she was never briefed about the CIA's use of the waterboarding technique during terrorism investigations. The CIA produced a report documenting a briefing with Pelosi on September 4, 2002, that suggests otherwise. Judicial Watch also obtained documents, including a CIA Inspector General report, which further confirmed that Congress was fully briefed on the enhanced interrogation techniques. Aside from her own personal transgressions, Nancy Pelosi has ignored serious incidents of corruption within her own party, including many of the individuals on this list. (See Rangel, Murtha, Jesse Jackson, Jr., etc.)

Rep. John Murtha (D-PA) and the rest of the PMA Seven: Rep. John Murtha made headlines in 2009 for all the wrong reasons. The Pennsylvania congressman is under federal investigation for his corrupt relationship with the now-defunct defense lobbyist PMA Group. PMA, founded by a former Murtha associate, has been the congressman's largest campaign contributor. Since 2002, Murtha has raised $1.7 million from PMA and its clients. And what did PMA and its clients receive from Murtha in return for their generosity? Earmarks -- tens of millions of dollars in earmarks. In fact, even with all of the attention surrounding his alleged influence peddling, Murtha kept at it. Following an FBI raid of PMA's offices earlier in 2009, Murtha continued to seek congressional earmarks for PMA clients, while also hitting them up for campaign contributions. According to The Hill, in April, "Murtha reported receiving contributions from three former PMA clients for whom he requested earmarks in the pending appropriations bills." When it comes to the PMA scandal, Murtha is not alone. As many as six other Members of Congress are currently under scrutiny according to The Washington Post. They include: Peter J. Visclosky (D-IN.), James P. Moran Jr. (D-VA), Norm Dicks (D-WA.), Marcy Kaptur (D-OH), C.W. Bill Young (R-FL.) and Todd Tiahrt (R-KS.). Of course rather than investigate this serious scandal, according to Roll Call House Democrats circled the wagons, "cobbling together a defense to offer political cover to their rank and file." The Washington Post also reported in 2009 that Murtha's nephew received $4 million in Defense Department no-bid contracts: "Newly obtained documents...show Robert Murtha mentioning his influential family connection as leverage in his business dealings and holding unusual power with the military."

<u>Rep. Charles Rangel (D-NY)</u>: Rangel, the man in charge of writing tax policy for the entire country, has yet to adequately explain how he could possibly "forget" to pay taxes on $75,000 in rental income he earned from his off-shore rental property. He also faces allegations that he improperly used his influence to maintain ownership of highly coveted rent-controlled apartments in Harlem, and misused his congressional office to fundraise for his private Rangel Center by preserving a tax loophole for an oil drilling company in exchange for funding. On top of all that, Rangel recently amended his financial disclosure reports, which doubled his reported wealth. (He somehow "forgot" about $1 million in assets.) And what did he do when the House Ethics Committee

started looking into all of this? He apparently resorted to making "campaign contributions" to dig his way out of trouble. According to WCBS TV, a New York CBS affiliate: "The reigning member of Congress' top tax committee is apparently 'wrangling' other politicos to get him out of his own financial and tax troubles...Since ethics probes began last year the 79-year-old congressman has given campaign donations to 119 members of Congress, including three of the five Democrats on the House Ethics Committee who are charged with investigating him." Charlie Rangel should not be allowed to remain in Congress, let alone serve as Chairman of the powerful House Ways and Means Committee, and he knows it. That's why he felt the need to disburse campaign contributions to Ethics Committee members and other congressional colleagues.

****

Big government means different things to different people. However, some believe BO is going overboard. He really believes his is KING and warrants all these perks:

If you're not sure what "big government" implies, take a look at this . . ..

COMMENTARY

An entourage surpassing the queen's

President Obama showed up at the G-20 summit in London with everything but the proverbial kitchen sink — although he did bring the White House chef and the kitchen staff.

DALE MCFEATTERS

Dale McFeatters writes for Scripps Howard News Service.

The heads of government in London for the G-20 summit are discussing serious and weighty issues, which in time will be duly reported on, but right now the British press is entranced by the sheer size of President Obama's traveling entourage. And no wonder.

Obama arrived with 500 staff in tow, including 200 Secret Service agents, a team of six doctors, the White House chef and kitchen staff with the president's own food and water.

And, according to the Evening Standard, he also came with "35 vehicles in all, four speech writers and 12 teleprompters." For sure, our president is not going to be at a loss for words.

The press duly reported on Air Force One and all its bells and whistles but also on the presence of the presidential helicopter, Marine One, and a fleet of identical decoys to ferry him from Stansted airport to central London.

Among all those vehicles is the presidential limousine, which one local paper mistakenly called Cadillac One, but is universally referred to as the Beast. The limo, reinforced with ceramic and titanium armor, carries tear gas cannon, night-vision devices and its own oxygen and is resistant to chemical and radiation attack. It is, marveled one reporter, a sort of mobile panic room. The Guardian called it "the ultimate in heavily armored transport."

The president is entitled to all the security, communications and support he feels necessary to do his job but surely, when we're trying to project a more restrained, humble image to the world, the president's huge retinue could be scaled back to something less than the triumphal march from "Aïda."

But you have already read about this in your local newspaper ..

Oh no, you didn't? OK then, you saw it on CNN... No?... INTERESTING!!!

You and I may never again see health care the way it used to be, but "Emperor Obama" took six (6) doctors with him for a 3 day visit to   London   - along with 494 other essential staff.

****

They may be your first family but they sure aren't mine.

Kind of makes one wonder????????

Stupid is, as stupid does

As any American knows, we place our right hand over our heart when we recite the Pledge of Allegiance.

And for anyone who thinks this may be a mirror-image picture, please note the wedding rings on the ring fingers of their LEFT HANDS and the RIGHT side of the Messiah's suit coat where the buttons are.

These two morons are so clueless they can't possibly be Americans!

Summation

**

Robert A. Hall is the actor who plays the coroner on CSI if you watch that show. He is much more than an actor. Read to the end.

This should be required reading for every man, woman and child in the United States of America.

"I'm 63 and I Tired"

by Robert A Hall

I'm 63. Except for one semester in college when jobs were scarce and a six-month period when I was between jobs, but job-hunting every day, I've worked, hard, since I was 18. Despite some health challenges, I still put in 50-hour weeks, and haven't called in sick in seven or eight years. I make a good salary, but I didn't inherit my job or my income, and I worked to get where I am. Given the economy, there's no retirement in sight, and I'm tired. Very tired.

I'm tired of being told that I have to "spread the wealth" to people who don't have my work ethic. I'm tired of being told the government will take the money I earned, by force if necessary, and give it to people too lazy to earn it.

I'm tired of being told that I have to pay more taxes to "keep people in their homes." Sure, if they lost their jobs or got sick, I'm willing to help. But if they bought McMansions at three times the price of our paid-off, $250,000 condo, on one-third of my salary, then let the left-wing Congress-critters who passed Fannie and Freddie and the Community Reinvestment Act that created the bubble help them with their own money.

I'm tired of being told how bad America is by left-wing millionaires like Michael Moore, George Soros and Hollywood Entertainers who live in luxury because of the opportunities America offers. In thirty years, if they get their way, the United States will have the economy of Zimbabwe, the freedom of the press of China, the crime and violence of Mexico, the tolerance for Christian people of Iran, and the freedom of speech of Venezuela.

I'm tired of being told that Islam is a "Religion of Peace," when every day I can read dozens of stories of Muslim men killing their sisters, wives and daughters for their family "honor"; of Muslims rioting over some slight offense; of Muslims murdering Christian and Jews because they aren't "believers"; of Muslims burning schools for girls; of Muslims stoning teenage rape victims to death for "adultery"; of Muslims mutilating the genitals of little girls; all in the name of Allah, because the Qur'an and Shari'a law tells them to.

I'm tired of being told that "race doesn't matter" in the post-racial world of Obama, when it's all that matters in affirmative action jobs, lower college admission and graduation standards for minorities (harming them the most), government contract set-asides, tolerance for the ghetto culture of violence and fatherless children that hurts minorities more than anyone, and in the appointment of U.S. Senators from Illinois.

I think it's very cool that we have a black president and that a black child is doing her homework at the desk where Lincoln wrote the Emancipation Proclamation. I just wish the black president was Condi Rice, or someone who believes more in freedom and the individual and less arrogantly of an all-knowing government.

I'm tired of a news media that thinks Bush's fundraising and inaugural expenses were obscene, but that think Obama's, at triple the cost, were wonderful; that thinks Bush exercising daily was a waste of presidential time, but Obama exercising is a great example for the public to control weight and stress; that picked over every line of Bush's military records, but never demanded that Kerry release his; that slammed Palin, with two years as governor, for being too inexperienced for VP, but touted Obama with three years as senator as potentially the best president ever. Wonder why people are dropping their subscriptions or switching to Fox

News? Get a clue. I didn't vote for Bush in 2000, but the media and Kerry drove me to his camp in 2004.

I'm tired of being told that out of "tolerance for other cultures" we must let Saudi Arabia use our oil money to fund mosques and mandrassa Islamic schools to preach hate in America, while no American group is allowed to fund a church, synagogue or religious school in Saudi Arabia to teach love and tolerance.

I'm tired of being told I must lower my living standard to fight global warming, which no one is allowed to debate. My wife and I live in a two-bedroom apartment and carpool together five miles to our jobs. We also own a three-bedroom condo where our daughter and granddaughter live. Our carbon footprint is about 5% of Al Gore's, and if you're greener than Gore, you're green enough.

I'm tired of being told that drug addicts have a disease, and I must help support and treat them, and pay for the damage they do. Did a giant germ rush out of a dark alley, grab them, and stuff white powder up their noses while they tried to fight it off? I don't think Gay people choose to be Gay, but I damn sure think druggies chose to take drugs. And I'm tired of harassment from cool people treating me like a freak when I tell them I never tried marijuana.

I'm tired of illegal aliens being called "undocumented workers," especially the ones who aren't working, but are living on welfare or crime. What's next? Calling drug dealers, "Undocumented Pharmacists"? And, no, I'm not against Hispanics. Most of them are Catholic, and it's been a few hundred years since Catholics wanted to kill me for my religion. I'm willing to fast track for citizenship any Hispanic person, who can speak English, doesn't have a criminal record and who is self-supporting without family on welfare, or who serves honorably for three years in our military.... Those are the citizens we need.

I'm tired of latte liberals and journalists, who would never wear the uniform of the Republic themselves, or let their entitlement-handicapped kids near a recruiting station, trashing our military. They and their kids can sit at home, never having to make split-second decisions under life and death circumstances, and bad mouth better people than themselves. Do bad things happen in war? You bet. Do our troops sometimes misbehave? Sure. Does this compare with the atrocities that were the policy of our enemies for the last fifty years and still are? Not even close. So here's the deal. I'll let myself be subjected to all the humiliation and abuse that was heaped on terrorists at Abu Ghraib or Gitmo, and the critics can let themselves be subject to captivity by the Muslims, who tortured and beheaded Daniel Pearl in Pakistan, or the Muslims who tortured and murdered Marine Lt. Col. William Higgins in Lebanon, or the Muslims who ran the blood-spattered Al Qaeda torture rooms our troops found in Iraq, or the Muslims who cut off the heads of schoolgirls in Indonesia, because the girls were Christian. Then we'll compare notes. British and American soldiers are the only troops in history that civilians came to for help and handouts, instead of hiding from in fear.

I'm tired of people telling me that their

party has a corner on virtue and the other party has a corner on corruption. Read the papers; bums are bipartisan. And I'm tired of people telling me we need bipartisanship. I live in Illinois , where the "Illinois Combine" of Democrats has worked to loot the public for years. Not to mention the tax cheats in Obama's cabinet.

I'm tired of hearing wealthy athletes, entertainers and politicians of both parties talking about innocent mistakes, stupid mistakes or youthful mistakes, when we all know they think their only mistake was getting caught. I'm tired of people with a sense of entitlement, rich or poor.

Speaking of poor, I'm tired of hearing people with air-conditioned homes, color TVs and two cars called poor. The majority of Americans didn't have that in 1970, but we didn't know we were "poor." The poverty pimps have to keep changing the definition of poor to keep the dollars flowing.

I'm real tired of people who don't take responsibility for their lives and actions. I'm tired of hearing them blame the government, or discrimination or big-whatever for their problems.

Yes, I'm damn tired. But I'm also glad to be 63. Because, mostly, I'm not going to have to see the world these people are making. I'm just sorry for my granddaughter.

Robert A. Hall is a Marine Vietnam veteran who served five terms in the Massachusetts State Senate.

****

Another poem that touches at the heart of what most of us are thinking:

**

Why is it people want to hide
And no one seems to tell
Why all our precious oil
Is gushing from that well?

Why can't all the engineers
And President's smart men

One Candle at a Time

Put the B.P. oil wells
Back together again?

I think it is bad politics
That has taken place
Obama blames Republicans
So he can save his face.

Any simple person
Would know just what to do
Drill another well by it
Diverting all the GOOO !!..
. . . OR . . .
SHRED OBAMA'S HEALTH CARE PLAN
AND MIX IT WITH SOME GLUE
IT WILL SEAL IT OH SO TIGHT
AND SOLVE BOTH PROBLEMS TOO

Barbara Cook

****

Thanks Barbara.

During the last few years the citizens of this great nation have been put through the ringer. Not only has the BO administration dealt us dirty, but the many natural catastrophes that have happened is enough to make one wonder.

Maybe God is trying to tell us something. We have earthquakes, fires, tsunamis, wars, tornados, hurricanes, terrorists and more and we still believe that we are in control. We are being given a warning that the last days are upon us and we need to shape up - quickly.

I know for sure that I don't want to roam around the desert for 40 years without knowing where were headed. I know my path and I plan on following it until the end. No one can tell me that the entire universe was created by the "BIG BANG" unless you also state that God created the BIG BANG. There is no way that all these things just happened.

There is only one candle I wish to see and that is the light from Jesus's candle which lights the world.

I wish to thank all those that sent me so many emails. I hope that I have done them justice in this book.

I also hope that I have not stepped on anyone's foot or taken something out of context or copied some copyrighted article. Most every article was widely circulated and in the "public domain".

I thank you again for supporting my efforts in making our feelings widely known (I hope).

Ron